Stoning the Keepers at the Gate

Stoning the Keepers at the Gate

Society's Relationship with Law Enforcement

Lawrence N. Blum, Ph.D.

Lantern Books • New York
A Division of Booklight Inc.

2002
Lantern Books
One Union Square West, Suite 201
New York, NY 10003

Printed in the United States of America

Library of Congress Cataloging-in-Publication Data

Blum, Lawrence N.
    Stoning the keepers at the gate / Lawrence N. Blum.
        p. cm.
ISBN 1-59056-006-X
1. Police—United States—Public opinion. 2. Public opinion
—United States. 3. Police—United States. 4. Law enforcement
—United States.   I. Title.
HV8139.B58 2002
363.2'093—dc21

2002013068

To my Paula, Noah, and Nicole.

Y por esos vivo.

Acknowledgments

I met a police officer while standing on line at a bakery in Los Angeles, and we began to talk about policing in today's society. He told me sadly that he had been forced into officer-involved shootings twice in the seven years he has been working to protect his city. His comment saddened me as well: "At the end of it all, I felt like a suspect." I have heard the same feelings expressed over and over again by other officers across the nation during the talks I give—hence the motivation to write a book that aims at understanding and rapprochement between the American public and its police officers.

This work is the culmination of a twenty-plus-year career spent on the battlefield that is police work in contemporary American society. I use the word *battlefield* because that is precisely what a majority of police officers experience each and every time they don the badge and perform their duty. Whether their combat takes the form of an assault against them by a "two-strike" parolee found to be carrying a gun or drugs, or the broad-brushed condemnation of their actions in prolific media reports following a controversial action, too many police officers continue to be disillusioned, wounded, alienated, and killed as part of the price they pay to fulfill their mission: to protect others from predation and attack.

The outpouring of public appreciation following September 11, 2002 and its celebration of police officers and firefighters gave me hope for a prolonged rapprochement that would permit society to obtain a real understanding of the influences that determine the quality of police work. This book is an attempt at contribution toward those ends.

I was motivated to write this book more by an appreciation for the daily acts of police heroism that I have witnessed that the public will never hear about, than by any of my clinical experience or biases that I have developed regarding police training, supervision, and leadership that will be discussed in the book. I could never begin to count up the sum total of those individuals in law enforcement who have taught me so much about selflessness, heroism, altruism, and honor, as well as how a police agency can be torn apart. I still have not determined if this knowledge is a blessing or a curse.

The book is indebted in large measure to the police experts who were sought out and interviewed for this work, and to those of my clients who have permitted me to share their stories with a public who they feel does not trust them. Their agreement was based upon my request that they allow me to show the public some of the realities and consequences of performing police work with excellence.

I thank my friend and partner, Sergeant Ed Deuel, Huntington Beach Police Department, for teaching me so much about the day-to-day experience of working police officers, and providing me with access to police life that ordinarily would not be available to an "outsider."

Kasey Geary of the Anaheim Police Department, while not the only police officer I have worked with who was shot and severely wounded, taught me what courage truly means. He was shot through the jaw, neck, and brachial plexus while attempting to investigate illegal drug and gun sales, and fights through daily pain to perform his work. I recently learned that Kasey was called to the residence of a mentally troubled woman who had obsessively collected all of her trash since 1941. She was forced to live in her backyard, because her entire house was literally filled to the brim with trash.

Kasey transported her to a hospital and let the doctors and nurses know that he was committed to seeing that this tragic person received maximal help until such time as he "worked some things out for her." On his own time, and using his own money and personal influence, he formed a group of volunteer providers who removed over twenty-three tons of trash from her home. He personally got the house back up to compliance with city building and safety codes, got a plumber to volunteer to put in a new water main, and put new plumbing and fixtures in the home. From others, he collected new furniture and a new bed for this woman whom he did not even know. How sad that the national news media do not find actions like his newsworthy.

Detective Mike Nakama and the other members of the Huntington Beach Police Department Major Crimes Against Persons Unit taught me how relentless police work can save lives threatened by organized gangs of bank robbers and murderers. Detective Mike Reilly from Huntington Beach Police Department fought for years to remain on the police force after he was diagnosed with a highly dangerous injury in his thoracic vertebrae. His efforts saved the life of an innocent kidnap victim who was about to be executed.

Sergeant Robert Essen, Supervising Officer, Los Angeles County Sheriff's Department Academy, was of great help to me in learning about the trials and tribulations of turning today's youth into expert deputies under very difficult conditions. Mike Willis, Whittier Police Department (Ret.), and Officer Joel Willis, Anaheim Police Department, demonstrated the tradition of service and mission within a family. Both father and son are recipients of the highest award available to police officers for service above and beyond the call of duty, the Medal of Valor.

Officer Art Tintle, Garden Grove Police Department; Officers Hannah Campos and Alisa Salcido, South Gate Police Department; Senior Officer Stacy Lim, Los Angeles Police Department; and Lt. Charles McCarthy, Los Angeles County Sheriff's Department provided an invaluable insight into police work through their experiences.

Sheriff William Kolender, San Diego Sheriff's Department; Sheriff Leroy Baca and Undersheriff William Stonich, Los Angeles County Sheriff's Department; Chief G. "Steve" Simonian, Los Angeles County District Attorney's Bureau of Investigation; Randy Narramore, Huntington Park Police Department; and Chief Joe Polisar, currently Vice President of the International Association of Chiefs of Police and Chief of the Garden Grove Police Department, have all taught me that excellence in police work is attainable with effective leadership performed by persons of great character and courage to "do what is right" for both their officers and the communities that they serve.

I thank the staff of Lantern Books for their support. Finally, I thank the working police officers throughout this country for taking care of us even as we "stone the keepers at the gate."

Table of Contents

Introduction

It was a night in Los Angeles, about ten years ago. A prowler had been victimizing the residents of a senior citizen mobile home community in the city. A police officer searching for this prowler observed a figure standing by the doorway of a mobile home. As the individual neither attempted to enter the home nor left the front doorway, the officer decided to "check out" his purpose for being there. Then the figure standing at the doorway raised a pistol and shot at the police officer, who reacted according to his training and will to survive by returning fire, wounding the suspect.

The officer took the suspect, who turned out to have victimized a number of elderly citizens over a period of years, into custody and arranged for his transfer to a hospital for medical care. The suspect wore a neoprene sleeve around his knee, such as joggers wear to lessen the impact of running. The headline in the local newspaper blared, "Cop Shoots Disabled Person!"

The officer agonized over the newspaper reporting of the incident. "I didn't shoot any disabled person. This guy shot at me in the act of breaking-and-entering into an elderly person's home. Why didn't they tell the truth?" The news story made it appear that he had acted out of control and injured an innocent, disabled person. The officer felt betrayed and fearful—how would he be perceived and treated now? Would this newspaper story be used against him if he had to use force in a subsequent incident?

There are currently thousands of police officers who feel some degree of alienation from the people for whom they risk their lives. They are fearful that if they act according to their training, they will be unfairly judged to have done something wrong. Many officers have reported to me the feeling of anger and betrayal at always being portrayed as the "bad guy" in the media when they take police action. They believe that most of the public buys into the negative image of police often presented by the media and has no idea what police work requires.

Even after the outpouring of affection and respect that showered police personnel following September 11, 2001, there continues to be an expectation on the part of a large number of police officers that they will be punished for performing their job (Blum, 1998). This is largely because injurious misunderstanding and misinformation have distanced the public and police from each other. The primary purpose of this book is to fight this historic trend of decreasing trust and mutual respect between the police and the public by shedding light on some of the factors that strongly affect the contact that society has with its police officers.

The debate over the use of aggression by police officers is an important one for society to learn more about. A number of contemporary police officers may feel some reluctance to put their hands upon a threatening individual, either because of a fear of unfair scrutiny and criticism, or because of the risk of personal civil liability. As will be discussed in detail below, it is my contention that such reluctance or delay will actually result in the risk of greater police force being used, because the officer who loses the initiative to an assaultive person will experience an instinctive urgency to "catch up" to protect them from the threat.

During the horrifying attacks against the United States by terrorists on September 11, 2001, the country experienced the reality of criminal violence *en masse*. We learned of the actions taken aboard a hijacked airplane by some of its passengers that caused the plane to crash into a field instead of, perhaps, the White House or Capitol building. Americans embraced the actions the passengers took to save those who would otherwise have died—actions that required the application of violent force. The passengers had to impose their wills upon the hijackers in order to thwart their mission. I was struck by the unanimity of that public response to violence. Perhaps it was the unbelievable scale of the devastation, or the catastrophic change in our view of our safety and security, that inspired such vast support for greater enforcement measures to combat threats against America.

Society has worn blinders to the fact that terrorist acts have been perpetrated frequently in American towns and cities since long before September 11, 2001. These were attacks by Americans on the fabric of American society. For example, the gang and drug infestation in urban and suburban communities has altered the manner in which schools function and children are reared. Children, especially in urban and impoverished rural areas, have observed violence, death, drug dealing, and predation since they were old enough to see. There have been many funerals for toddlers killed in "drive-by shootings," shot by bullets meant for other gang members.

Perhaps we don't see a public demand to fight the predators in our own communities because the victims are counted one at a time, or tend to live in disenfranchised communities that do not attract the media attention that the tragic murders of, for instance, Ennis Cosby, the Menendez family, or Nicole Brown Simpson and Ronald Goldman were given. Whatever the cause, it is this book's contention that society has been making a dreadful mistake in how it prioritizes demands for law enforcement efforts in the United States.

I must admit to a bittersweet taste as I witnessed the outpouring of support for the police officers who gave their lives during the terrorist attacks against our country. In the weeks following September 11, many in America participated in ceremonies to honor the heroism demonstrated by public safety personnel during and after the attack. These individuals ran in the opposite direction from the people fleeing the World Trade Center buildings. They ran toward the threat, not from it, and, in doing so, gave their lives in the attempt to save the innocent victims.

These were the same police officers who had been vilified just the day before: "They're not trustworthy. They overstep the bounds of authority. They lie, they cheat, and they abuse people." Indeed, there are policies in police work today that are built upon the mistrust of officers and prohibit them from using their discretion in a number of important conditions, apparently in fear that, left to their own decisions, they would do something to create liability for their department. For example, a number of agencies have specific prohibitions about a patrol officer's involvement in an investigation with a child victim of thirteen years of age or younger. In other agencies, officers are prohibited from attempting to halt a fleeing suspect in a vehicle pursuit by what is termed lawful intervention (e.g., causing the suspect vehicle to spin out by gently turning the left front quarter of the police unit into the right rear quarter of the suspect vehicle) regardless of what threat a fleeing individual causes pedestrians and other motorists.

The message given to officers is that the very department and people they are risking their lives for do not trust them. I have observed countless heroic acts by police officers over the twenty years I have served as a police psychologist. But society's response to them before September 11 was most often to "wave at them with one finger raised in the air."

Why, if we feel anguish at the death of over 300 law enforcement officers in the attacks against America on September 11, 2001, do we seek actions in police officers that are less decisive and vigorous in dealing with locally threatening circumstances—thereby placing both the officer and the subject of the police response at much greater risk?

This book will try to answer the above question and to present some solutions. It will explore the causes and conditions behind society's mistrust of law enforcement, and show how that mistrust can lead to tragic consequences. And it will shine a light on areas usually hidden from public view—including the training, professional and political pressures, and mental and physical lives of police officers—that can tip the balance toward life or death for officers and the citizens they have sworn to protect.

1. Attitudes toward Law Enforcement in American Society

It has been my experience that people tend to hold strong beliefs about law enforcement. All of us have deeply embedded feelings about authority figures that stem from our familial, peer, and other relationships. These in turn have an impact on the way we perceive individuals whom we, as a society, allow to hold positions of authority. The complex sources of that dynamic and the way they express themselves can be seen in the following example of a resident of Louisville, Kentucky, who explained how the police were viewed in his community:

> There has been such a negative view of the police. People don't trust them. . . . And most of those who are policing us do not live in our area so, therefore, they don't understand what we're going through. . . . So, there's a lot of misunderstanding . . . no communication at all. . . . That's the kind of attitude [distrust of the police] that the community has . . . . Attitudes are learned . . . So for twenty years they're taught that the police are no good. . . . You know, it's a lot of hard work to get somebody to change their perspective of

7

something like the police department all of a sudden when you've been taught all your life to think a certain way about them. (Rosenbaum, 1994, p. 45)

Because our perceptions and judgments are determined by our own attitudes and values, people's evaluations of police officers and police work in their communities normally have very little to do with the performance standards within the department. I have listened to harsh, critical comments made about "cops" and been struck by how little most people know about the realities of policing. Denial of the harsh, violent, or dangerous aspects of the world is a commonly used psychological defense that allows us to go about our lives without constant fear of harm. If we were unsuccessful at "blocking out" unpleasant parts of our world, the horror we would feel each day at the violence and suffering that are always taking place would overwhelm us. We depend upon the police to keep such horrific sights, sounds, and smells away from our lives and our experience of the world.

Our ignorance can be catastrophic, however, for police departments, individual officers, and their families. Here is one such story.

Members of a large local urban police department referred John to me when he was having substantial difficulty performing his duties as an officer. When I saw him, he recounted an incident that later turned out to have been the beginning of the end of his career.

He and his partner were following an El Camino (a vehicle that looks like a pickup truck in the back and a passenger car in front) that was occupied by two males who were acting suspiciously. The vehicle would drive very slowly until it approached an intersection. The driver would speed up to take the corner, then slow down again. The officers ran the license plate on their vehicle's computer, and the car came back as having no arrest warrants attached to the plate. Nor was it listed as stolen.

John and his partner tried to determine the reason for the driver's strange behavior. They believed that the individuals in the car ahead of them were either attempting to toss drugs or a gun out of the car, or were surveying the police vehicle for a possible "set up." The area they were patrolling was plagued by gang and drug activity and was felt by the residents to be a war zone between the two major gangs vying for control of narcotics sales.

The slow pursuit continued until the vehicle that the officers were following made a sudden stop. The top of the vehicle popped open. A man rose suddenly like a jack-in-the-box and began firing a gun into the windshield of the police vehicle. This man was wanted for violent crimes by a number of local, state, and federal law enforcement agencies.

The windshield of the police vehicle imploded, sending shards of glass flying into the car. The officers dove out and away from their vehicle to gain better protective cover from incoming bullets.

The driver of the El Camino remained at the wheel while the passenger leaped out and ran down an alleyway in an apparent attempt to evade the police officers. John got out of the car and ran in pursuit of the fleeing suspect.

After several seconds in pursuit, he saw the suspect rise suddenly from behind a bush at the side of the alley and again point a gun at him. This time, however, John was prepared for the attack, as he had already been fired upon and was in a mental and physical state of combat readiness. He fired his service weapon just before the suspect fired his own gun.

He saw the suspect react as if he had been punched. The man dropped to the asphalt, and John heard and saw the suspect's gun clatter to the ground approximately two to three feet from the suspect's body. "Thank goodness," he thought. "It's over. He's mine."

But it wasn't over. The suspect, who had been struck in the torso by the officer's bullet, began to crawl toward his gun. John repeated the same command over and over: "Stop, don't do it. . . . Let it go. No one has to get hurt. This doesn't have to happen. You don't have to do this. It's over. Don't make me shoot you. Don't make me shoot you. Please don't make me do this!"

Asking this suspect to abandon his intention to kill John (rather than return to prison for his "third strike") was like asking a scorpion not to sting its prey. John felt helpless. "What does it take to stop this guy?" he thought. No matter what he did, he was unable to end the threat. "Bullets are supposed to stop people, and this guy isn't stopping."

The suspect kept moving toward the gun lying upon the asphalt. His hand was about to close around the grip area of the fallen handgun when the officer fired four more times. John's second fusillade of bullets ended the fight.

The suspect stopped moving toward the gun; the physical threat had ended. The man began to curse at the officer, and fought with the paramedics who arrived soon afterwards. John and the paramedics provided emergency first aid to the suspect to keep him alive. Later that evening, John was told that one of his bullets had entered the suspect's back and partially severed his spinal cord. He was going to be paralyzed from the waist down.

In the aftermath of the shooting, John did not experience any sense of relief at having survived the lethal series of assaults. Nor did he gloat over his victory. In fact, he was horrified that he had caused such severe physical damage to another human being. It didn't help that some of his fellow officers seized upon this opportunity to call him "back shooter" and other phrases used in police humor as a way of dealing with the trauma of violence.

When John got home the next morning, his two sons ran to greet him with the same glee and excitement they always showed at his arrival. In the past, John had always rushed to his children upon arriving home and scooped them into his arms. But today, though he had no idea what had changed in him or why, he recoiled from them. He thought, "How can I put these hands on my two sweet boys when they have caused such damage to another person?" He thought of himself as stained, unclean. He did not want to infect his sons or his wife with the feelings of guilt that surged through him.

This officer was a devoted member of his church and had volunteered in numerous youth activities there. He was committed to providing care and safety to the people who lived in the beat he patrolled, even though many there expressed dislike of his uniform, feeling that it symbolized an unfriendly society. He had a powerful conscience and sense of fair play. He felt a personal, moral, and ethical obligation to serve others.

He now feared that the suspect's fellow gang members would attack his family in retaliation for shooting one of their own. He began to see danger everywhere he went. He became angry and withdrawn. He stopped going to church, believing that his feelings of discomfort meant that he no longer belonged there. He spent months in treatment with me in an attempt to return to being the person he felt he had been prior to the shooting.

Over time, John began the road back to healing. He came to understand that his feeling of great sadness was a logical reaction to the tragic nature of the incident. He learned that many police officers, when they experience helplessness while something terrible is happening, develop inappropriate feelings of responsibility for what happened, because "we're supposed to control every event we come in contact with." He learned to separate his feelings of sadness at something terrible having happened—a healthy and logical reaction to the incident—from the inaccurate and destructive belief that he was to blame for saving his own life against a man who would have made his children fatherless.

But the impact of this incident upon his life was not over. The man who had twice ambushed this officer with murderous intent brought a civil lawsuit. To show solidarity with his gang and proclaim his loyalties, the man painted his wheelchair blue, the color symbolic of a criminal gang called the Crips. The plaintiff's contention was that he had not ambushed John in the alleyway, but had been on his knees in the middle of the asphalt, attempting to surrender to the officer who had come upon him. He claimed that the officer had ignored his pleas to allow him to give up. He said that he had never tried to hurt John, but that the officer had moved behind him while he was on his knees and had shot him "execution-style in the back."

The plaintiff's own expert witness (who made a substantial living testifying against police officers in court cases regarding officer-involved shootings) agreed that his claim could not be accurate given the entry and line of the bullet's passage. However, social attitudes toward the police in post–Rodney King Los Angeles were then characterized by mistrust, fear, and alienation. A jury of citizens awarded $4.6 million to the wounded Crip, whose criminal history revealed a continuation of violent crimes against other persons, and who had been shot while attempting to murder a police officer. Members of the jury later said that they felt that a message had to be sent to the police. Effectively, however, they had determined that John had violated this individual's civil rights simply by defending himself against a predator.

John never recovered from the damage done to him by this court decision. He left his family, became estranged from his wife and children, and removed himself from the community he had served so loyally. Gone was the loving dad who had devoted every waking moment off duty to his family and his church.

He couldn't accept the fact that the jury had not believed him. He had testified accurately and honestly about what he had done during the incident. He couldn't understand how the very citizens he worked so hard to protect had perceived him as an evil person, a representative of those to whom a "message had to be sent."

John could no longer perform police duties. He was preoccupied to the point of obsession with ongoing fears that he would be involved in another shooting and have to go through the same experience again. His senses and judgment were interrupted by nightmarish visions of the shooting and the announcement of the jury's verdict. He constantly imagined gang members coming after his children for revenge. He suffered through a severe and prolonged depressive disorder created by great feelings of loss—of his career, his self-esteem, and his relationship with his family—the kind of depression that is difficult to extinguish through psychotherapy because it is based upon current, real-life events.

His mental and emotional condition was so severe that he was forced to retire from police work. He could no longer "pull himself together" to perform his tasks. He was clearly emotionally distraught, and his constant preoccupation with the event prevented him from concentrating on anything else.

He received a medical disability retirement. The injury that had forced him to retire was hard for him to explain to the many people who asked him about why he was no longer a police officer. After all, there were no broken bones or entry wounds from a bullet to show to those who wondered why such a young man was out of work. His wound went straight through to his inner soul.

While it is now years since the court decision was made—December 28, 1998—I still fear the phone call that may reveal this officer's final, self-destructive response to the wasteland that his life became.

The reason behind the real-life nightmare that destroyed John—as it has many others who work in today's law enforcement—is simple. It has to do with the way society very often perceived police officers prior to September 11, 2001, and the heroism of public safety personnel that was demonstrated on that day.

On September 11 and in the days following the terrorist attack, New Yorkers, along with the rest of America, stood on sidewalks and cheered the police who passed by carrying out their duties. Did September 11 make police officers more trustworthy than they had been on September 10? How could the guardians of our society—the police—have been so maligned?

Society has not gauged the increasing consequences of failing to support the work of police officers, not only when great tragedy strikes but each day, when officers place themselves in the line of fire to protect ordinary citizens such as you and me from the worst criminals among us. It's time to examine the causes and consequences of the problems that have faced the law enforcement community in the ten years since the video of Rodney King was flashed around the world. The problems can be evoked simply with a catalogue of names: O.J. Simpson, Abner Louima, Tyesha Miller, Amadou Diallo, Rampart.

There has been important progress in law enforcement made in response to social demands. However, I have also observed the genuine concerns felt by society over police activity being twisted by defense lawyers attempting to lessen the credibility of evidence against their clients, sensationalized by a media hungry for controversy, and distorted by citizens who do not realize that, in their blanket condemnation of law enforcement when scandalous actions are committed by a few, they are condemning the very institution that protects them and their right to life, liberty, and the pursuit of peace and happiness. They are stoning the keepers at the gate.

Where do society's beliefs about law enforcement and police activity come from? In addition to childhood experiences and learning, people base their beliefs and attitudes upon information they receive from sources they find credible. In large measure, contemporary society receives its news from television, newspapers, and talk shows.

One of today's most ubiquitous and influential information sources is the television news. Attractive, photogenic journalists and presenters smile out of the television set, often communicating their personal attitudes along with the news via their comments, facial expressions, and demeanor. Naturally, we are drawn to attractive people; we want to identify with them, and we tend to believe them.

14

We feel that they are friendly and warm toward us, so we want to like them.

What we see and hear every day becomes familiar to us; what is familiar we perceive as normal, and our brain becomes conditioned to think in this manner. It should not be surprising, then, that societal attitudes are influenced by the way the news is presented—whether it is the news organization's political agenda or its need to sensationalize something for increased ratings and greater advertising revenue. The news media is, above all, a business, and must capture and hold the public's attention.

If one were to count the media reports of police work throughout the nation in the ten years prior to September 11, 2001, one would observe a distribution of story content skewed significantly toward a critical view of police officer activities. Before September 11, the media was full of stories about racial profiling and police brutality. After September 11, that type of coverage came to a dramatic halt. Instead, numerous media reports described the heroism, selflessness, and generosity of police officers. Clearly, all these supposedly brutal, corrupt police officers could not have been magically transformed into heroes without a great deal of "bandwagon" reporting—coverage that sought to play into people's worst prejudices regarding the officers who protect them, or their desire to cheer for the heroes who are seen working to save them.

"Bandwagon" reporting creates a skewed public view of police officers that either encourages hostility toward them or denies the real and considerable dilemmas facing law enforcement today. In either case the public is denied a true analysis of the influences that shape law enforcement. Any distortion or inaccuracy in media accounts may affect people's perception of what society must to do to solve some of the problems facing the police.

The public's view of law enforcement is also influenced by day-to-day contact with police officers. An article in the *New York Times* related the following event:

It was a little after 4 o'clock last Tuesday afternoon, and two teenagers had just been shot to death at Church Avenue and Raleigh Place in Central Brooklyn. As the police descended, the curious gathered behind yellow crime-scene tape. . . . On one side of the street, a police officer apologized to the growing crowd—mostly West Indian immigrants—for closing off Raleigh Place. "It's a crime scene," he said. "Just bear with us. It's for everyone's benefit." A mother and her three children waved to him. He waved back. . . . Across Church Avenue, another officer told people to move along. "This street's closed—you can't cross," he said abruptly. A nurse in aquamarine scrubs cursed him loudly before reversing course. . . . Two officers, two sides of the street, two images of the force. That the police would arrive to protect and investigate was assumed. What they were being judged on, then, were their interactions with the crowds at the yellow tape. (Waldman and Cooper, 2001)

Waldman and Cooper performed sixty-five interviews in the neighborhoods from the north Bronx to central Brooklyn, several months after Abner Louima settled his lawsuit with the City of New York for damages incurred when he was arrested and tortured one night inside a Brooklyn police station. While the views expressed in these interviews cannot be generalized to all persons, they do bear witness to the types of attitudes some city dwellers have toward their police department. Waldman and Cooper wrote:

Some said that to their surprise, they had seen shifts in attitudes and behavior: officers trying to be more polite, and stereotype less, at no cost to public safety. More, though, lamented that despite the outcry of the last few years, they saw no improvement, and not just in terms of discourtesy.

Many black and Hispanic men complained that they were still being stopped, searched and bothered without cause. And some—mostly, though by no means all, women and white men—said they had so little direct contact with the police they could not draw a firsthand impression....As crime continues to drop, fewer people report their fear that the police will not perform the duties at the heart of their work. What matters, the interviews suggest, is the manner in which those duties are performed. The snap, personal judgments formed during the briefest of encounters can be lasting and therefore influence the broader debate about the Police Department's character and conduct. (Waldman and Cooper, 2001)

Social attitudes about policing have long been studied, with several researchers and authors identifying the following factors in civilian beliefs about law enforcement: race and ethnicity, gender, socioeconomic condition, political affiliations and beliefs, education, geographic location, and age.

In the majority of studies (Brodeur, 1998; Guyot, 1991, Yarmey, 1990; Bailey, 1989; Bayley and Mendelsohn, 1969), people who were characterized as having authoritarian personalities were found to have positive opinions about the police because they saw them as their allies. Likewise, in general, the more politically and socially conservative views a person held, the more favorable was his or her opinion of the police. Older people, too, generally held positive attitudes toward the police. In fact, senior citizens had more positive attitudes toward the police than toward trial judges, prosecutors, and defense attorneys (Yarmey, p. 123). It seems logical to expect that persons more likely to need assistance from others would be more directly conscious of the benefits afforded them by the police.

Children are usually quite positive about the police, and "their praise is appreciated because it is sincere" (Guyot, p. 280). Indeed, it is relatively simple to perceive the source of children's comfort with police personnel. Children are more directly and consciously aware of their fears for their safety and well-being than are adults. The police officer or deputy sheriff's proximity creates the sense of security and safety for the child that his or her environment may have failed to produce or extinguished through violence and danger.

People of color were more likely to be dissatisfied or less satisfied with law enforcement than whites. Persons living in rural and suburban areas and neighborhoods were more likely to feel positive toward the police than those in urban neighborhoods, particularly those areas within the city that were poor.

There are many people in ethnic communities who believe they are poorly treated by the police (Friedman and Hott, 1995; Federal Bureau of Investigation, 1992; Walker, Spohn, and DeLone, 2000). At least three major riots in the 1990s, as well as a number of public demonstrations of rage, occurred following uses of force by primarily white police against primarily African-American or Hispanic subjects.

There are also conflicting attitudes within minority communities about the police. A 1996 survey documented that a large majority of people of color had little contact with the police, and complained that they did not receive adequate police protection (Federal Bureau of Investigation, 1992). Still others within disadvantaged communities believe that police officers spend too much time unnecessarily bothering people of color. Racial problems, gang violence, the homeless, and mentally disordered persons create problems for law enforcement. But they are also reflective of general social problems in America. It is demonstrably naïve to expect the police to provide solutions to social problems that have, in actuality, more to do with economic, political, and social class than ethnicity or violations of law.

It is likely that many more people felt positively toward the police before September 11, but had not been as vocal as those who were critical. Nevertheless, the fact remains that unless members of society now learn to become more informed consumers of police services, those services are likely to suffer in a way that will increase the danger and distress to citizens as well as officers. In the next chapter, we'll look at how this has already happened.

2. Changing Attitudes, Changing Times

> There has been a big change in the culture of policing in the past few years, as lifestyle becomes more important than the sense of public service . . . (Butterfield, 2001)

Maria had been a police officer for about eight years. She worked as a member of a team of officers that patrolled a specific geographic area of the city. Her team was comprised of three male officers beside herself. While Maria had always performed well and "pulled her weight" on patrol, she continued to feel the same pressure that many women in law enforcement experience from male officers—no matter how many times she had already proved that she could perform police tasks as well as the men, she constantly felt the need to prove it again in order to gain acceptance and respect as a police officer.

One night, she was serving as a cover officer (responsible for supporting or backing up the officer or officers who are in direct contact with a subject) for two of the male officers on her team who were placing a person under arrest. The police had had a number of prior contacts with this subject and his family, who were known for continual involvement in disturbing and possibly criminal activity within their jurisdiction.

The two male officers, referred to as contact officers because they were responsible for the direct contact with the subject of police action, were handcuffing the suspect's wrists when he decided that he did not want to be arrested that night. The officers had positioned and locked one of the restraints around the individual's wrist when he broke from their physical control. The other steel handcuff and chain hung free from his hand.

Predators of all varieties have a general rule of thumb: when their intended prey appears to be vulnerable, smaller, weaker or more helpless than they are, they attack. When their prey is aggressive, or appears stronger or more powerful than they are, they withdraw or flee.

Maria weighed almost one hundred pounds less than the individual who was attempting to avoid apprehension. He instinctively attacked her by holding the free-hanging steel handcuff and chain like a bludgeon, striking her with all his strength on the side of her head and at her eye. He then grabbed her with his hands around her throat and began to try to choke her to death.

The blow that defeats us is never the hardest blow we take; it is the one we do not see coming. This attack was totally unexpected and stunned Maria momentarily. She was unable to draw breath because the attacker's hands were closing her airways. She told herself over and over again not to allow the man to take her down. But the criminal dragged her to the ground by placing his much larger body upon her and throwing her backwards, with her head and neck at the point where the curb separates the sidewalk from the road. With his hands still around her throat, he lifted her head and then smashed it down on the curb, over and over again.

Maria was in danger of losing consciousness due to a severe concussion. She was terrified by her inability to breathe. She felt her eyes bulging as if they were going to leap from their sockets. Her tongue was pushed out of her mouth. Her skin tone was changing to a bluish tinge. Maria knew she was dying.

The faces of her two young children came suddenly into her mind's eye. She was a single parent and was the only person who cared for her two boys. Without her, she knew, they would have no one to put them in their pajamas, comfort them when they were frightened, take them to school, and help them grow up to live a good life.

She fought to stay alive not because of any conscious decision, nor was it because she feared for herself. She refused to surrender to death because her two young sons needed their mommy. She kept thinking and moving, acting purposefully, the most critical actions an officer must take to save his or her own life after being shot, stabbed, or bludgeoned. (Blum, 2000). She succeeded in forcing her fingers into a wedge between her assaulter's hands and her neck. She kept turning on him, because she knew this was what she needed to do to stay alive.

The third officer on their team had approached, and now the three male officers stood above her and observed Maria's struggle against her assailant. "Where are they?" she thought. "Why aren't they killing him? I'm going to die! They're supposed to come and help me!" The male officers began only to pry at the fingers of this would-be murderer, an action that had no effect upon the attacker. They attempted no other uses of force to save Maria. Either she would save herself, by her will to fight and live, or she would die.

By the male officers' own reports, Maria was on the ground for a period of 60 to 120 seconds. It took her that long to reverse her position and get this individual—who had given her a severe concussion and multiple contusions, and had fractured her cranium—into a headlock and take him finally into custody.

Maria then overheard one of the male officers say to the other, "If we made him bleed like he made her bleed, then the liability's on us." All officers make a promise to protect their fellow officers, but that promise was not kept on this night.

More police officers began to arrive from other patrol sectors of the city and brought the assault to an end. Maria refused to be taken to the hospital. "I'm OK. I'm fine. I can handle this," was her groggy, confused response to paramedics' requests for her to lie down on their gurney. An officer who arrived at the scene following the assault took one look at her and ordered her into the ambulance. Maria was bleeding from her head and ears, her eyes and sinus areas were blackened, and she had multiple cranial contusions and a serious concussive injury to her brain.

News of this incident spread throughout the police department like wildfire. People were angry and began to point fingers in an attempt to make sense of what had happened. In the days following this event, other police officers began to cancel requests for backup assistance if one of the three male officers was assigned to assist them. A great deal of anger and mistrust was building, and the rumor mill was turning at high speed.

This police officer and her department had experienced a trauma and injury that could and should have been prevented. The incident raised issues of critical importance to the police officers and the health of the police agency. Officer safety had been compromised because some officers were more concerned with avoiding liability than with saving the life of their partner. It was incumbent upon this police agency to ascertain how it could have created conditions that had allowed such harm to come to one of its officers. There are always lessons to be learned from the debriefing of difficult, dangerous, or complex police activities. This incident raised a plethora of training, tactical, and integrity issues, and could have led to true progress within the agency in how its officers comported themselves under conditions of assault and threat.

This, unfortunately, did not happen. The chief of police was three months away from retirement. Perhaps he ordered the department and all its personnel not to talk about this incident because he wanted to create peace within the agency. Or it may be that he just didn't want to face the difficult issues that arose from admitting that police officers had been inactive, passive, and immobilized in the face of a lethal assault against a fellow officer. Whatever the reasons for the inaction or dysfunctional reactions to this event, the incident and the response are stark symbols of some of the negative aftereffects of the changes occurring within police agencies over the last twenty years.

No mention of Maria's injuries appeared in the media. She was a casualty kept secret from the public eye. No one explored the impact upon officer morale of a lack of support for each other in the field, and passive leadership at crucial points in a police agency's experience. Should the attempted murder and beating of a police officer not be as repugnant to society as a police officer's improper behavior?

Over the months that I have provided assistance to Maria, who continues her police work in spite of the daily headaches she may always endure as a consequence of Post-Concussion Syndrome, I continue to ask myself, "How have we come to this state in our society, when the keepers at the gate stand back, willing to risk the death of a good person in order to avoid the risk of liability? Is that the type of police response that society desires—one that protects criminals from police uses of force while officers are killed because they were insufficiently prepared for combat?" The public must be alert to the fact that the development of such passivity, hesitancy, or indecision in a significant number of police officers will place the innocent at greater risk of having to fend for themselves should they be the unfortunate victim of a criminal.

How might this happen? As a result of being trained, supervised, and ordered to alter their behaviors, attitudes, and habits to meet social demands for a more service-oriented police officer, many law enforcement agencies have moved away from the concept of a police officer that was held until ten years ago. Officers who are hired today very often define themselves less as crime fighters who put crooks in jail, and more as service providers who help their communities with a range of problems.

In many cases, the police have moved from a proactive style of policing—in which, for example, they would stop someone who looked suspicious to them—to a reactive, less confrontational or aggressive position in relation to criminals. This phenomenon does the public a disservice, and exists more to protect municipalities and counties from liability in lawsuits than to protect society.[1] Even in those departments where the role of crime fighter is still valued, the distressing consequences undergone by police officers who take action will influence many officers to de-emphasize the seeking and apprehension of criminals. Police officers, like any other human beings, will become defensive in the face of continuing stress and distress if they are not adequately prepared to face such pressure and are not supported properly in countermanding its dangers. In such conditions, performance inevitably declines.

A considerable number of officers have been greatly disillusioned by the way they have been treated following the performance of their duties. The attitude that police officers have about law enforcement is very important to society, because it is this attitude that will determine what levels of performance they demand from themselves. An officer's drive toward peak performance can be incapacitated through the loss of support, either from the public or, more often

---

1. In one California county, for example, several million dollars a year are spent in settling claims made against deputy sheriffs in order to avoid lawyers' fees and the cost of trials. As a representative of one major urban police department reported to a journalist, "The idea is to use computer systems to track information on officers and analyze statistical trends that might expose local governments to higher liability costs. For example, the Los Angeles Police Department hopes to have the software power to crunch such arcane bits of information as whether officers use twist locks or wristlocks. The LAPD and the city had long been criticized for being slow to develop such a system. Now, partly owing to the pressure from the Justice Department, we are taking this to a level no one has been at before," he said (*Los Angeles Times*, April 11, 2002).

than not, from their own organization. Police officers may well be disciplined or investigated within their police agencies if they use force against someone who assaults them. If they are involved in enough incidents in which force was required, or if the incident involved a politically sensitive encounter (such as a white police officer and a person of color), they can be perceived as possible "problem officers," likely to result in future liability for the municipality or county.

The impact of such a response by their agency has been devastating to many police officers who acted according to their training and the science of tactics. I have marveled at the level of "Monday morning quarterbacking" performed by those who scrutinize police officers with inadequate knowledge of the circumstances in which those officers acted. If those judging law enforcement actions do not possess a complete and accurate data base from which to evaluate police behaviors, then the validity of their evaluation is lessened to the extent that their pronouncements are based more upon personal and political values than on sound science.

An officer who delays or hesitates in his or her attempts to control an assaultive person where physical force is required will not receive scrutiny, and may well be rewarded (via promotion) for not drawing negative attention from outside the agency. The performance of police work by these individuals, however, does no great service to the public; these officers are not fulfilling their proper role as protectors of the community.

I was asked in 1999 to develop and implement a "training the trainers" program for a large urban police agency in southern California. The program was designed to help officers mentally prepare themselves for dangerous encounters, enabling them to act appropriately during unanticipated, rapidly changing, or chaotic conditions, using a range of force options from verbal requests all the way to lethal force.

One part of the training that all patrol officers in that agency participated in was a "suicide by cop" scenario in which a disturbed person assaults a police officer in a pathological attempt at suicide that is, unfortunately, not uncommon in contemporary society.

The science of tactics requires that, during a felonious assault against them, police officers must immediately adapt their use of police procedure to impose control upon the person committing the act of violence. In order to avoid being killed, officers must, at some point during the attack against them, recognize that verbal tools are not viable to control this threatening person, and that non-verbal control methods must then be applied decisively, lawfully, and according to procedure.

In this scenario, the role player begins the encounter by telling the trainee that he is not going to go back to jail, and then escalates the gravity of his actions by closing the distance between himself and the trainee. Almost one out of every two trainees limited their attempts to control the suspect—and protect themselves from harm—to increasing the volume with which they ordered the suspect to "Stop . . . stay right there . . ." When a trainee limited his or her efforts to control the suspect to verbal commands, the role player managed to close the distance between himself and the trainee (a definite "no-no" in police tactics), pulled a knife he had secreted in his jacket, and stabbed and killed the trainee.

The trainees knew that officers who take decisive, forceful actions consistent with the science of police tactics (see, for example, the tactics laid out in Heal, 2000) today are met with highly distressing consequences, even though such actions are appropriate and ethical. I have had a number of officers tell me during talks and lectures that they had allowed suspicious persons to continue unheeded, because they had decided to lessen their aggressive police response in order to avoid putting themselves and their families through the hell that many have experienced for doing their job as police officers. As one officer described the situation in *Force under Pressure: How Cops Live and Why They Die* (Blum, 2000):

> We often compromise our own safety to make the case. We don't want to be criticized in court or embarrassed by a weak report, so we give the suspect freedom to act so that we can justifiably react or justifiably search. In reality, we knew this person was dangerous from the moment we saw him, but we can't just draw our weapon and search people and their cars without probable cause. So we act cool and stupid and we don't call for backup when we should. We will look weak in front of our peers if we constantly call for backup. Yet, aggressive police officers are constantly hunting parolees. If I call for a backup too often I will get a nickname. If I don't call for backup when I should, I end up calling myself lucky. (Deuel, 1999)

A paradoxical condition exists today in a substantial number of police officers. While they rush into danger to save people by virtue of their heroic instincts during catastrophic events, they now often avoid probable cause contacts with suspicious-looking persons to lessen the chance of being punished for their aggressive search for criminals. As we saw earlier in the chapter, officers have even abandoned aid to a partner in imminent danger.

Today's police officers perform their work duties in an environment where "the actions of a few result in punishment for the many" (Bildt, 2002). Examples of this include the dismantling of the Major Narcotics Enforcement Unit by a former Los Angeles County Sheriff after members of that unit were caught stealing money, and of the Anti-Gang Unit in the Rampart Division of the Los Angeles Police Department after Rafael Perez was caught stealing cocaine. The loss of such efforts has resulted in a lessening of the amount of intelligence that patrol officers are able to use in high-crime neighborhoods—giving local gangs an advantage and resulting in a more dangerous local community.

It amazes me that the public has embraced proactive security efforts to protect Americans from terrorist actions, but eschews the same proactivity with local law enforcement efforts. At the time of this writing, American soldiers are on foreign soil hunting down terrorists, murderers who destroyed the lives of innocent people. The prevailing media reports upon the war are most often positive in their support of this effort needed to protect Americans. Why, then, does society react with dismay to a police officer's aggressive pursuit of local terrorists?

At least some portion of the public seems to harbor a mistrust of the motivation for police actions, and to fear corruption within the ranks. Similar concerns can and do exist within police organizations themselves, as was shown in 1999, when violent demonstrations accompanied the World Trade Organization meetings in Seattle, Washington.

I was asked to provide debriefing services to the police officers of a large urban police agency in the Northwest United States, who were reportedly experiencing a great deal of anger and distress following their encounter with violent, aggressive, and destructive behavior by demonstrators who had attempted to disrupt the World Trade Organization's conference in their city. I was told that the officers were not so much bothered by the fact they had been insulted and assaulted (in an obvious effort by the demonstrators' strategists to get a violent, visible response by the police) but were greatly upset at how the leadership of their department and city had behaved toward them. Even though I had been briefed on the likely reactions I would encounter in assistance to the officers there, I was totally unprepared for the level of distress these officers were subjected to by their mayor and their own department's leadership.

The police officers had been ordered not to respond to the demonstrators' actions, no matter what they did to police officers, but to hold their ground only. The officers, who were greatly outnumbered by demonstrators in the downtown area, were overrun, beaten, and spat upon. They had urine thrown on them and were kicked and cursed at for periods of twelve to sixteen hours straight without being provided with a single rest or break from the skirmish lines. Following orders, they did not return the aggression. The amount of restraint these young men and women had shown in response to the rioting was astounding to me.

They told me that the leadership of the city must have believed the statements of the demonstration organizers, who had met with the mayor and police chief prior to the conference, that the demonstration would be peaceful and non-destructive. Some of the officers in the audience were infuriated by the fact that their leadership had chosen to ignore intelligence that had been received and reported to the executive command of the department and city administration, to the effect that violence and disruption were part of the planned strategy of an international political group that had engaged in violent demonstrations in Europe during a prior meeting of the WTO.

This decision meant that officers were insufficiently prepared and equipped in materiel and practice time to prevent loss of life and property. For example, after a consultant had recommended to the police administration that they purchase close to eighty thousand dollars worth of chemical spray, a less lethal alternative to shooting, to cope with the expected demonstration, the city's police decision makers purchased only a tenth of that amount, requiring a police captain to fly to Wyoming *during the demonstrations* to buy more of the spray because the police had run out by the second day. An analogy could be made with a military unit that is sent into battle with insufficient ammunition and supplies against forces superior in number. The public is rarely made aware of the extreme psychological and physiological stress placed upon those who must face combat without the necessary resources.

When some of the demonstrators began to break the windows of the large Nike Town store in the central city on the second day of rioting, the police were ordered to take control. That the officers themselves had been assaulted for more than twelve hours non-stop had not warranted a command decision to permit the police to regain control of the city and protect themselves from violent assault.

Fortunately, very few of us are ever commanded to remain in a fixed and stationary posture while others scream threats at us and hurl jars of urine. Such self-control is contradictory to almost every normal human survival instinct and, if used for prolonged periods, can cause profound physical and psychological damage (Blum, 1998).

The department's leadership had demanded that field supervisors and commanders send all information and requests to a central command group prior to ordering or taking any actions against the demonstrators. Due to the amount of time it took to have the information communicated to central command, and to the amount of unlawful activity occurring, it was taking, on average, sixty to ninety minutes for a field supervisor to receive clearance to act upon the situation he or she had reported. In that time, the decision the central command staff sent back down had become irrelevant.

As I listened to the feelings of these embattled officers, I couldn't stop thinking, "If the chief did not trust his sergeants, lieutenants, and captains in the field to make the necessary decisions, why were these people promoted to ranks?" Fortunately for these police officers, many citizens made their affection and appreciation for these fine officers quite evident during all three days of disturbances. Some officers in the room told me that citizens had offered them sandwiches and thanked the officers for taking care of them.

That these citizens communicated their gratitude for what the police had done for them was of great comfort to these officers. I have for years found it ironic that, while most people view police officers as "hard, tough" people, the vast majority are very sensitive and

32

idealistic individuals whose feelings are greatly touched by signs of appreciation from those for whom they risk their lives.

The public must understand that in order to get excellence in policing, police officers must first be confident that the community they are risking their lives for will support their decisions. To the extent that this confidence does not exist, there will be some degree of degradation in the quality of policing that community receives. For example, many law enforcement officers today limit their actions primarily to responding to someone calling the police and requesting service. Such limitation allows criminals a much greater degree of mobility and freedom from apprehension, because the police who had hunted them may now feel reluctant to do so, or may be hamstrung by limited information made available to them via the dismantling of specialized units that engage in an aggressive pursuit of criminals.

For example, until four or five years ago, crime statistics in Los Angeles, California, like those in many other large urban areas, had been steadily decreasing. Recently, however, that pattern has changed, and violent crime statistics have risen sharply. Bernard Parks, the outgoing Chief of Police of the Los Angeles Police Department, in a speech to the City Council to protest his being denied a renewal of his contract (a denial attributed in part to a rise in crime statistics) blamed the rise in crime on the loss of patrol officers to community policing and other work assignments agreed to in a Consent Decree with the federal government (*Los Angeles Times*, April 10, 2002).

While I am not attributing the cause of rising crime statistics to police inactivity, the concern remains that a "pendulum swing" of change has resulted in a number of perhaps unintended consequences that do not serve society well. Society's concerns about police force must never reach the point that we become willing to risk the sacrifice of police officers in order to create a community-sensitive, service-oriented style of law enforcement that fails to prepare police officers for the highly dangerous circumstances and conditions they will encounter in the course of their work.

While it is absolutely necessary to protect citizens from improper or excessive police force, the current trend toward reluctance to act is not the answer. There are thousands of police officers who continue every day, with great effort and self-sacrifice, to reach out to or save people they do not even know. There is a tremendous effort being undertaken by many, many police officers and detectives who may find within their own agencies as many obstructions to the performance of their duties as they would find from the criminals they are pursuing.

In July 1999, four masked gunmen, members of the criminal gang called the Crips, committed an armed takeover robbery of a bank. They screamed, cursed, and pistol-whipped the customers and employees. One woman was sexually molested. The gunmen escaped with one hundred thousand dollars in cash. An electronic tracking device had been included in the cash given the robbers.

The police tracked the device to another city and, with the help of the local police agency, took the four gunmen into custody. They found and collected a great deal of evidence regarding this and other bank robberies by this gang. The police had had prior contact with two of the gunmen, who were considered bosses in the robberies. One was the mastermind who planned the crimes and identified the targets, and the other recruited members from among all the Crip gangs in California to participate in armed robberies and murder. The detective told me that the mastermind was connected at high levels in the criminal underworld, inside and out of prison. All four had spent a number of years in prison for armed robbery.

The detectives had captured one of the most active and violent bank robbery crews in the Southwest. These crooks, under the direction of the mastermind, were "good" for more than forty bank robberies from San Diego to Clovis, California (in the central part of the state). Some time after their arrest, a bank in Bakersfield, California was robbed by members of the same gang. A gun battle erupted between the police and the bank robbers, and a detective who shot and killed one of the crooks was later threatened with death.

The detectives who followed and arrested the bank robbers found out about the robbery in Bakersfield and connected the crew who had attacked their city with the later robbery. The criminals' method of operation also connected them with many bank robberies in other states.

The detective unit contacted the Bakersfield Police Department, which was unaware of intelligence about gang members in southern California. The Bakersfield detectives told them that gang members had flooded the courtroom during the trial of a fellow member in an obvious attempt to intimidate everyone involved in the trial. The detectives from the southern city felt an urgent need to help Bakersfield police because, as one told me, "There were heavy players still out and planning more. . . ."

They contacted their lieutenant to request permission to go to Bakersfield and provide critical intelligence to the detectives there, especially involving threats against the life of the Bakersfield detective who had shot and killed the robber. The lieutenant said he could not understand why they "needed to go up there." He asked the detectives if they had to stay overnight in Bakersfield, and expressed concern about the cost. The information they had was contained in several boxes, each of which held hundreds of pages of important documents known to the local detectives through cooperative intelligence sharing in the southern region of the state. The detective who told me this story looked at me with an embarrassed expression and said that the lieutenant had asked them, "Why can't you meet them halfway?"

The detectives presented their case. The criminals they had apprehended were connected to many serious crimes. The lieutenant's response was: "Those other crimes didn't happen in [their city]."

The detective told me that he and his team had worked over a period of several months, resolving many bank robberies committed by this group of criminals for many other police agencies. They felt a strong sense of accomplishment at what their efforts had brought about, but were absolutely dismayed at their department's response to their request for support for their mission. The detective was also shocked that detectives in some other agencies were satisfied just to work local cases "while these criminals had never been held responsible. . . . Now there is a chance to hold them accountable."

He told me that he feared that witnesses to the mastermind's upcoming trial would be executed. He said that they had been working for years on this group of interconnected cases "and my commander is concerned only with 'counting beans,' if we need to stay over."

The detectives decided that they would travel to help Bakersfield; if their own department would not pay for the trip, they would pay for it themselves. Desiring to focus upon their efforts to bring down a prolific gang of violent criminals, they were instead burdened with matters that seemed trivial in contrast to the crimes they were investigating. When the detectives arrived, the locals laughed at the "big city" detectives who were being watched like school children with a strictly monitored allowance. The detectives' embarrassment did not dissuade them from showing the local detectives how to work this case with their information when the mastermind came to trial.

Now the detective's eyes lit up as he said to me, "[The mastermind] got word that we were coming. . . . He has informants, like any other major criminal. . . . He pleaded guilty to fifty-eight years to life." He felt vindicated.

This detective and his team continue to work this and other serious cases with their eyes on one purpose: to get the worst crooks off the streets to protect society. The public should not permit such dedication to be damaged by efforts at police reform and budgetary efficiency.

Of course, efforts at police reform are not in themselves bad. One example of an excellent new program can be found in Los Angeles, where Sheriff Leroy Baca has turned a jail facility into a treatment program for men convicted of domestic violence and some types of drug abuse. His deputies work directly with the inmates in both a custodial and remedial capacity. This program has had unusually high levels of success with these offenders; however, it, too, is being closed due to budgetary concerns (*Los Angeles Times*, April 16, 2002).

But Sheriff Baca continues to exert his influence as a forward-thinking leader in the way he runs his department. He told me that he is dissatisfied with a system that forces one to choose between a service-oriented deputy and a "crime fighter" orientation. In his mind, his deputies are leaders in the community. He views their role as encompassing essentially all types of services needed by local communities, from Head Start to incidents requiring Special Weapons and Tactics units.

If we demand the kind of excellence in police work that has been suggested by Sheriff Baca, we must provide police with the proper tools and the right organizational and social environment in which to achieve it. Our police officers must be equipped with the most modern technology available today—and, for the most part, they are not. The tools that they carry on their belts are two-hundred-year-old technology. The new technology that would greatly enhance how officers perform on difficult or dangerous assignments is denied them because of budgetary constraints (Simonian, 2002). In a number of agencies, for example, patrol officers must delay their use of less-than-lethal weapons with a resistive or assaultive suspect because only supervisors possess such munitions. In other departments, like the one in the above story, police officers may not be provided the resources and supplies necessary to achieve excellence in police work. Less-than-lethal munitions have saved scores of assaultive suspects whose actions would have otherwise resulted in the need for police to use lethal force. To deny all officers the necessary equipment, training, and resources because of budgetary constraints suggests the misapplication of funds by city and departmental decision makers.

As will be discussed later, officers must also be trained with methods that actually re-create the conditions they will encounter in the field. Reform must include a strong emphasis upon making police officers better decision makers under stress, and trusting them to make such decisions based on the conditions that they have encountered—not on a preoccupation, for example, with being unfairly scrutinized for using force, or on an inflexible predisposition to a community service orientation that precludes the use of force even when warranted.

Officers must be supervised and led by individuals who have proven their ability to lead and to create a drive toward excellence in those who follow them—not by people who hold leadership positions because of gender requirements or political affiliation within the agency. Finally, and most importantly, they must be properly supported in their work by the public and by their own organizations.

These types of support are crucial to the achievement of excellence in law enforcement, and will be discussed in greater detail below. There is another vital element, however, over which the public has no control: the individual officer's innate ability and character. The qualities the officer himself or herself must contribute are the subject of the next chapter.

3. The Making of Police Officers

We citizens want police officers who act with honesty and integrity. We want officers who obey the rules just as we have to do. We want officers to treat us with professionalism and respect. We want officers to be sensitive to our values and cultural diversity. We don't want racists or bullies. We want officers to be disciplined in the performance of their duties. We don't want them to harm people unnecessarily. We want them to serve us; after all, we pay their salaries. We want them to control their emotions, language, speech, and behavior in order not to offend us. We want them to act as community servants and provide us with assistance in solving social problems that occur in our communities. We do not want them to act as if they are an occupying army. We want them to separate criminals from us so that we may live in comfort, free from fears of victimization by predators.

Most people today would likely agree with the above picture of how police officers should comport themselves. When we encounter individuals in a police uniform, we expect them to act according to our idea of what a good police officer is and does.

The tasks performed within police work are quite varied, and range from participating in a neighborhood improvement committee to calming a potentially suicidal person into accepting treatment instead of death, to protecting the innocent and vulnerable in society by finding, apprehending, and incarcerating the guilty. When you see a police officer performing with excellence and integrity, he or she will extend a gentle and kind touch to a community in need or a child who is lost—and take whatever actions are necessary to vanquish a threatening foe. The same person will do both, and more. The goodness of these officers' actions is not a response to scrutiny, mandates, or commands. It is a function of their character.

Integrity, Responsibility, and Character
While it is relatively simple to identify characteristics of excellence in police officers, it is more difficult to actually develop such excellence. We can, however, identify some of the elements of character that form the potential for excellence in law enforcement, and a good basic recipe will include integrity, responsibility, and character.

The manner in which individuals comport themselves in any work setting—and in police work in particular—will be, in large measure, determined by their moral and ethical values. While it is fairly easy to "look good" when one is being watched, the person with integrity must possess a strong sense of right and wrong, and live by this sense when it is difficult to do so. He or she must make his or her actions and behaviors conform to the requirements of law, policy, and honor, even when it is a personal sacrifice to do so.

Officers with integrity demonstrate a self-initiated willingness to be responsible in how they work and live. Responsibility means that individuals recognize and accept the obligation to correct faults they may have, or to work on areas within themselves that need improvement. It also indicates a commitment to fulfill the obligations they take upon themselves. Responsible people do not cut corners in order to make things easier on themselves, because the proper performance of the task requires that they continue with a sequence of actions that may not be comfortable for them. The lack of a demonstrated commitment to be responsible for one's actions does not bode well for the level of integrity a candidate will show as a police officer.

For example, a surprising number of applicants I have screened in pre-employment psychological evaluations have declared bankruptcy prior to their thirtieth birthday. They had purchased goods on credit because, they told me, they "wanted the good things in life," even though they had not yet reached the point in their life when their level of income and their discipline in managing their finances meant that they could afford those "good things." Later, when it came time to pay for what they owed, they sought legal means through bankruptcy laws to avoid the responsibility they had brought on themselves but failed to bear.

Interestingly, such a "blot" upon an individual's personal financial history has often been accompanied by an investigator's discovering that the applicant had also falsified or omitted information on his or her application that would have placed him or her in a critical light. When I have queried such individuals during the pre-employment psychological evaluation as to why, for instance, they had lied about the number of times they had smoked marijuana, or how often they had received criticism or discipline from an employer, their response was predictable: "I was afraid that I would be disqualified, and I want this job."

These are the individuals who as police officers are more likely to betray the trust of society, because their motivation to protect themselves from being criticized or facing up to the consequences of their actions will be more likely to overwhelm their commitment to honesty and integrity in reporting upon facts and events later in their career. The term used in law enforcement circles when an officer corrupts an honest reporting of facts out of a desire for secondary gain—for example, in order to make an arrest without legally obtaining probable cause—is "testilying." Much of the scandal, for example, caused by Rafael Perez and other members of the Anti-Gang Unit in the Rampart Division involved allegations that they sought secondary gain when they falsified and planted evidence on suspects they believed were guilty, in the absence of sufficient evidence to arrest these suspects properly.

Officers may have experienced frustration time after time when individuals they have arrested and strongly believe to be guilty are released from culpability due to a technicality, for example, in the law defining rules for search and seizure of evidence. Honorable and motivated individuals within police ranks are often disillusioned early in their career as they watch criminals smirk at the justice system and walk out of the courtroom door on a technicality. Or they have seen juries who are prejudiced against a police officer or deputy, disbelieve his or her report, and find instead for the criminal regardless of the facts of the case.

Officers and deputies may believe that an individual is guilty of some heinous act of rape, murder, or torture, but must follow strict limits in how they attempt to bring such an individual to justice—rules that, unfortunately, the criminal is not required to follow. It is ironic to many police officers that the very Constitution (and Bill of Rights) that they are willing to die for so values individual rights that the criminal gains advantage from the very laws that he or she violates. Some officers have been found to alter their reporting of the circumstances that permitted them to gather incriminating evidence against someone they believed to be guilty. They rationalized their act of falsification of reports because "the criminal got what he finally deserved."

The vast majority of quality police officers know that you can still catch the crook and do it "by the book." One does not have to sell one's honor to achieve convictions, even if good police work cannot accomplish them at a particular moment. As one officer said, "I am out here every night waiting. . . . I'll get him another time because he will be out here every night committing his crimes . . . ." (*MSNBC Investigates*, 2001).

In contrast to those applicants who try to hide their past actions and avoid responsibility for how they have comported themselves, I have known candidates for police work who live on bare subsistence at the same young age because they are "paying the piper" for their earlier, impulsive spending. They are determined to pay what they owe, because their conscience is too strong for them not to do so. Although these individuals "messed up," the fact they hate what they did, freely acknowledge their mistakes, and are motivated to improve themselves shows both integrity and responsibility. These individuals do not seek to avoid negative consequences for their actions. They accept these consequences as a valuable (albeit painful) lesson, and move on to greater achievement. They do not attempt to avoid taking the necessary steps to discipline and control their actions, to improve their performance and the quality of their lives. These individuals have the personality, habits, and desire that we should demand in each and every member of the police organization, from the brand new recruit to the chief executive officer. They should be driven by the need to serve, not the desire to place themselves in a more advantageous position within the organization. There should be no compromise in this area. This is the meaning of character.

One of the most important reasons that a background investigation and polygraph examination are performed with each police or sheriff applicant is to determine the applicant's character—for it is character that primarily determines the quality of a police officer. It is character that ensures compliance with rules and policy when no one is looking. It is character that helps a person stay in control through the tough times often encountered in the course of performing police duties (Stonich, 2002).

Character is a primary "fuel" for self-discipline and self-control under chaotic or dangerous circumstances. It permits the individual to perform acts of bravery and courage in the face of danger that the average citizen will never be forced to confront. One cannot possess integrity without character. One cannot escape the racism endemic in American society without character. One cannot withstand the temptations of the street without character. Without doubt, an individual will be unable to perform with the qualities demanded of police by society without strong character. It is through character that honor is developed.

An unspoken but necessary ingredient of honor is that the individual sacrifices his or her personal desires for comfort, gain, or position and acts for a higher good or purpose. The American Heritage Dictionary (2001) defines honor as "principled uprightness of character, personal integrity, a code of integrity, dignity and pride." Honor is observable in the acts that people describe as heroic. I have used a simple definition of "hero" when I have addressed police officers in classes I have taught: "Heroes are people who know that they can be harmed if they engage some dangerous or threatening condition, and yet they do so to save someone they do not even know."

Honor cannot be developed when the actions of police officers or their leadership are self-serving. For example, many chief executive officers serve at the pleasure of a three-to-two vote of the city council. The ongoing political processes inherent in local as well as federal governments are concerned with the possession, trade, and use of influence. The chiefs in such municipalities are faced with the possible consequence of being removed if they stand up for a position that is not sought by the majority of the council members. It is a rare leader indeed who possesses the honor and strength of character to withstand the immense pressure that is placed upon chief executive officers to "go along in order to get along."

If a chief of police is more motivated by the need to protect his or her position in the political arena of his or her municipality than by the commitment to stand up for what is right on politically sensitive issues, the officers under his or her command will have the tendency to model that same pattern of behavior (Bandura, 1986). If the chief takes a position because he or she believes that it is the right thing to do, even in politically sensitive situations, the officers under his or her command will model that type of performance as well (Narramore, 2002 and Polisar, 2002).

Maturity

The term "maturity" does not refer to a person's comportment at a party or in other social settings, or to the type of jokes he or she enjoys. It refers to how a person thinks, how he or she uses judgment, and whether or not his or her decisions are based upon objective facts rather than internal emotional states or needs. While many confuse maturity with life experience, these concepts are actually quite different. Life experience is something one can gain while one is learning how to perform police work. Maturity is a character trait that permits one to properly assess consequences prior to engaging in some action, as well as to conform one's behaviors to the formal and informal requirements of the work setting.

Officers who permit their personal idiosyncrasies, personality, or expectations to influence their work can place themselves or the subjects they contact in greater danger than if they had reacted objectively to the external conditions that they encountered. In most of the confrontations that have resulted in officers being murdered, or taking forceful action that was later viewed as improper, those officers had been in the process of attempting to place someone under arrest. An officer who, for example, takes insults or resistance from a subject as a personal affront will be highly likely to react with greater agitation, irritability, or anger than someone who does not, and may escalate a situation that a calm, commanding demeanor could have otherwise defused into an incident requiring physical force. Conversely, officers who perceive themselves as caring individuals, people who look for the good in others regardless of the type of person they are in contact with, will place themselves in a position that has already cost the lives of too many well-intentioned police officers (California Commission on Police Officer Standards and Training, 1996).

Police officers must determine if there has been a crime committed at the scene they encounter. They must identify how the different individuals present at the scene are reacting to their presence. They must determine what positions will be advantageous

45

to them if a tactical response is called for, and what positions will place them at a disadvantage. They must determine what resources they need to resolve the circumstances appropriately. Then they need to decide what tactics will be necessary and proper in this instance based upon the policy of the police agency, the training they have received, and their prior experience with similar conditions as police officers.

They must perform these tasks under extreme time compression. Critical decisions must be made as the incident is unfolding, in less than one second, with no opportunity to "take a time out." Unfortunately, many mistakes have been made, some of them tragic and catastrophic, in those cases where police officers were mentally unprepared for what they encountered, and therefore engaged in an action that was inappropriate given the conditions.

Maturity in a police officer means that one will be capable of purposeful and controlled adaptation to rapidly changing, unfamiliar, unanticipated, or chaotic events. Mature officers are capable of perceiving another's response tendencies and reactions to their presence immediately upon contact. Mature officers will base their approach to the individual upon their accurate analysis of the circumstance they have encountered and the resources that are available. They will also be capable of and predisposed to postponing their need for personal gratification until the appropriate time and condition.

The ability to postpone the immediate gratification of one's needs or desires is an important sign of mature adult development and mental health. For police officers, maturity often means resisting the immediate impulse—for example, to chase a fleeing individual down a darkened alleyway—until they have ascertained that the conditions they are likely to encounter are within their ability to control by themselves. If a mature officer determines that running after the suspect would place him or her in unacceptable danger, he or she will contact other officers to form a perimeter of containment in order to safely and effectively apprehend the criminal.

If someone asked a police officer to leap head first into a swimming pool without first seeing if there was water in the pool, he or she would likely scoff at the idea. And yet, many officers who have been murdered, or have engaged in uses of force that were found in violation of policy or law, leaped into the fray without first determining that they possessed the proper resources and preparation for such action. The ability to mediate how officers discharge their internal impulses to act (think of a gas pedal on one's emotions) is, therefore, the difference between life and death in law enforcement.

Adaptability

The vast majority of police actions involve the officer or deputy reacting to some situation that is already occurring or has already occurred. Very few of the millions of police actions taken in the United States are predictable. The officer or deputy must, upon observing the elements of a scene, assess the conditions, appraise the severity of threat and/or imminence of danger, and then decide how to best respond. He or she must immediately adapt his or her demeanor and actions appropriately to the requirements of the scene.

For instance, a neighbor-to-neighbor conflict or the search for a lost child may follow a high-speed chase of suspects. From the officer, the first event requires wisdom and patience; the second, compassion and reassurance; and the third, a readiness to use lethal force if necessary. The skills required of police officers in the performance of their work can, of course, be learned. What cannot be learned, however, are the internal psychological resources that enable officers to "shift gears" while still maintaining poise and control over their actions and demeanor.

The officer with effective skills in adaptation can demonstrate controlled responses during emotionally charged and possibly dangerous conditions to maintain order and calm. The adaptive officer can change his or her interpersonal demeanor in a variety of social encounters without any uncontrolled emotional reaction—whether it be intimidation or excess aggression.

The officer or deputy who demonstrates excellence will adapt immediately to both areas of mental and behavioral tasking (either defusing a situation through a quiet, relaxed approach, or taking aggressive action to seize control from a dangerous suspect) without the need for a mental "time out" to re-orient himself or herself or to regroup. The deputy or officer who is rigid or inflexible, and thus ill equipped to "shift gears" upon recognizing the needs of an encounter, will be incorrect in his or her response to most of the conditions that he or she encounters. This is true of both the officer whose tendency is to be brusque and curt with individuals as a matter of habit, and the one whose tendency is to show care and concern for individuals no matter how a given individual is behaving.

The alteration or adjustment of one's demeanor, behavior, attitude, or thought to an environmental condition or stimulus is termed in psychology an *adaptation response*. Fear, desire, rage, anxiety, vacillation, or impulsivity must not be permitted to intrude upon an officer's controlled response. But adaptability is necessary both during and after a dangerous encounter, as the following story will illustrate.

Stacy had returned to patrol duties after four years of working in gang and vice enforcement on a plainclothes detail. He had always been the type of officer who worked hard, constantly looking out for bad guys, writing traffic citations, and making arrests. He was determined that he would work no differently during this assignment. He had been back on patrol less than one month when he went to work on July 10, 2001.

During his time on vice unit duties, he had become aware of a nightclub that he believed was the site of regular narcotics dealing and the sale of alcohol to minors. He began to investigate the club but was forced to withdraw: "I was instructed that an ex-city councilman hung there. I vowed to return there when I hit patrol."

As soon as he returned to patrol, he began visiting this establishment on Saturdays and Sundays, citing violations that he observed. On one occasion, the security guard who worked at the club notified the officer that "There's this guy that goes in the parking lot behind the bar and sells dope and guns." The security guard was unsure about the exact description of the dealer's van.

Stacy parked one street away and began to survey the parking lot. He saw nothing for a couple of weekends while he attempted to seek out this person for questioning. On July 10, he had just left another bar he had gone to in response to a report of a fight that had occurred there. He received a computer message from a fellow officer who was at the nightclub Stacy had been working so intently. The message alerted him to a number of violations that were occurring. The officer who sent the message feels guilty to this day.

It was graveyard watch, Sunday morning at 1:45 a.m. Stacy pulled into the exit ramp area of the parking lot so that he could observe all the vehicles that were now leaving the nightclub. The security guard approached his vehicle, pointed to a Ford Explorer leaving the lot, and identified this vehicle as carrying the suspected drug and gun dealer.

"The guy in the Explorer sees me start to follow him and pulls in front of a 7-11 and walks into the store. . . . That's common for D.U.I.'s [persons driving under the influence of alcohol or drugs] to make me think they weren't driving," Stacy told me. "I black out [shut all the lights on his vehicle] and go around a car wash to get this guy. . . . I felt challenged by his behavior. . . . He comes out and drives away. He has tinted windows, which is a violation, and I think I have a D.U.I. . . . "

Stacy had made the assumption that this individual was not the person he suspected of drug and gun dealing, but "just a drunken driver." He put on his top red bar lights to signal to the motorist to pull over. The driver of the Explorer did not comply. Stacy observed him weaving slightly and in active discussion with a passenger. He decided that if the driver moved to the nearby freeway, he would cease his pursuit and transfer this incident to the Highway Patrol.

The Explorer was now stopped at a stoplight. Stacy shined his spotlight on the driver and noticed that he was "fidgety." His actions raised the proverbial hairs on the back of Stacy's neck. Stacy sensed something amiss and decided not to let this one go, so when the truck began to enter the on ramp to the freeway, he followed it. Immediately, the driver pulled the truck to the side of the on ramp and stopped. It was here that the man in the truck had decided to ambush Stacy.

"My intuition bells go off. . . . It's a limo tint so I can't see well. My spotlight is on his side view mirror. I see him do what no one does . . . he's staring intently, looking at me instead of avoiding the glare of the light."

The subject's actions had placed Stacy in an uncomfortable position. Instinctively, he immediately exited the police car and decided to approach the truck carefully on the passenger side. As he did so, he saw the right rear window opened about three inches. Stacy was unsure about what was happening: "Is this just a drunk, or is this going bad?"

Stacy stopped and peered into the space of the opened window. As he did so, he found himself looking down the barrel of a .45 caliber gun in firing position. "It was the biggest gun I ever saw in my life. . . . He said something to me—I've never told anyone that; I don't know what it was. Then he shot me."

Stacy had always planned what he would do if he were attacked. When he saw the gun, he immediately moved back and down (as evidenced by the trajectory of the bullet's path in his body) out of the suspect's sight picture. "He probably just leaned over, out the window, and shot me." The bullet entered at his jaw, shattered his jawbone, and then went through his neck into his brachial plexus, injuring the many nerves located in that area. It tumbled around his back and lodged in the soft tissue of his spine. The fall also shattered one of his vertebrae.

Stacy was placed on life support in the hospital and awakened three days later. He was given the best available medical care, but now lives and works with a slight paralysis in his left hand, arm, and leg. He is in daily pain from scar tissue in his jaw, brachial plexus, and neck that he will live with for the rest of his life. Most officers who sustain these injuries are faced with an extremely difficult decision: "Do I retire now, with benefits as a disabled person, or do I go back and do it again?"

For Stacy, there was nothing to decide. "When I hit the ground, I was looking at my feet, I felt myself bouncing, and I remember the first thing I thought was, 'Please, God, don't let me be so badly hurt that I can't be a cop anymore.'"

Stacy rehabilitated himself and returned to work. But his entire world had changed. He now found himself angered by things that had not bothered him before the shooting. He began having problems in his relationship with his wife, because he would explode verbally in anger at any frustrating condition or event. Crowded shopping areas or brightly lit places made him so agitated that often he would suddenly order his family to "get the hell out of here." He had no idea why all these emotional tornadoes were wreaking such havoc in him.

The officer was suffering the impact of Post-Traumatic Stress Disorder. A post-traumatic stress reaction occurs when officers experience unanticipated, extreme threat during encounters they did not expect. A *freeze frame* of a split second in time and space occurs, locking in the perception of the threat and extinguishing any alternative perceptions. In this manner, such incidents continue to seriously impact officers even though they have distanced themselves from the threat in time and space. What Stacy was experiencing as premonitions of "something terrible" if he was not always in control were actually flashback phenomena (intrusive recollections of the moment when the freeze frame occurred as he realized that he was being shot) that police officers are never trained in how to manage until after they are already wounded.

51

To Stacy's added dismay, the administration was greatly concerned about his readiness to return to work and instructed that he be evaluated for his fitness for duty. This was not a malicious act by his commanders. Most departments are unprepared to cope with wounded police officers, and often put them through unnecessary and distressing hurdles to prevent liability for the municipality.

While many in society are familiar with the term "trauma," few truly understand how such an event can impact an individual's subsequent life. Because trauma often results in a freeze frame perception, in which the split second that contained the major impact of the incident locks or rigidifies in the individual's memory and perceptions, any condition or circumstance thereafter that is similar to the traumatic event in any way is likely to produce the precise level of fear, alarm, sense of threat, and feeling of urgency or helplessness that were present in the original traumatic event. And because the individual has been traumatized, he or she is likely to experience much greater distress or dysphoria (discomfort) than ordinarily would have been caused by the new circumstances. He or she will focus his or her attention upon the currently occurring event, perceive the source of his or her great distress in the current condition, and therefore react inappropriately to the circumstances.

Stacy began to feel a growing sense of dread and a premonition of something terrible happening, even in situations that had elicited no such response in him prior to his being shot. His blood pressure was now elevated, even though he was being treated with medication, because his body was in a continuous state of alarm. Every situation in which he did not feel in control began to elicit flashback activity that left him alarmed, fearful, angry, and then drained and confused about what was happening to him.

Since that time, however, Stacy has worked with me to "make sense" of his apparently excessive reactions to everything. He has become more practiced in adapting to the new manner in which he interacts with the world. He has gained a great deal of control over his life, and continues to work in the darkness of criminal behavior and violence so that the residents of his city can sleep safely. His chief recently asked to speak with him. He told Stacy how much it meant to him that he had accomplished his comeback, and how he cherished his commitment and loyalty to the best purposes of law enforcement. I could not thank this chief enough, because he did more to heal this man in one hour than all of us "professionals" could accomplish in a month of treatment.

The point to be made here is this: if Stacy had not possessed the capability and preparedness to adapt immediately to confusing signals; the shock of violent wounding, pain, and disability; and then an altered approach to life after he was supposedly "OK" to work, he would never have made it. We must not permit officers to be at risk without preparing them through specific training and supervision to develop an expertise in effectively and purposefully altering their internal and external reactions to changing conditions, so that they can effectively respond to any and all circumstances that they encounter.

Communication

The ability to influence others is a critical component of police work. Therefore, police officers must be assertive and demonstrate effective interpersonal skills in all of their contacts with people. Officers must not experience emotional discomfort in anticipation of an interpersonal encounter, and they must not demonstrate an accompanying tendency to become anxious or insecure in how they deal with others.

Depending upon circumstance, an officer may take the role of a reasonable, logical, and helpful mediator, or assume a commanding presence that seizes control of a potentially dangerous situation by permitting nothing but compliance with his or her direction. Words alone cannot accomplish these tasks. Because most of the information in an interpersonal communication is transferred nonverbally, the officer or deputy also must communicate a presence. A commanding presence is of great importance in police work, given the nature of its most dangerous encounters. However, "command presence," while it assists officers in taking control of a situation, is in many ways antithetical to a service orientation in police work.

Communication is a reciprocal phenomenon, and its function in police work is not limited to officers or deputies expressing themselves in verbal and written form. The ability to receive, assess, and integrate information from the environment is of equal or greater importance for police officers. An officer must be able to "read" the conditions he or she will be required to control—whether a law has been violated, how a subject is reacting to his or her presence, etc.—and decide the appropriate response to the scene. The officer would fail the tasks of assessment, decision making, and applying the proper tactical response if he or she failed to integrate the information presented in the new situation with the learning and experience he or she has previously obtained.

A number of emotional conditions can and do disrupt a person's ability to use information in his or her environment, and/or to give information to that environment. This is so because emotional conditions are highly likely to disrupt the activity of the part of the brain that recognizes, decides, and judges—i.e., the "thinking brain" (Pitman, 1989; Van der Kolk, 1996; Blum, 2000). Think of a twelve-cylinder engine with only three cylinders receiving spark and fuel. This is exactly what happens in those parts of the brain responsible for observations, cognitions, analysis, prioritization, or reasoning when high-pressure, rapidly changing, unanticipated, or confusing events occur (Cannon-Bowers and Salas, 1998; Blum, 2000; Van der Kolk, 1996). The spark and fuel of brain activity is shifted to the more reactive (emergency) centers of the brain to fuel the alarm response (Everly and Benson, 1989; Pitman, 1989). During this transition, the "thinking brain" can be disrupted, distorted, or halted. The greater the intensity or emotion associated with some encounter with the environment, and the less prepared mentally the individual is for the encounter, the likelier this uncontrolled transition is.

Some of the personality traits that suggest the likelihood of a deficit in ability to perform vital communication tasks include perfectionism, impatience and irritation when others do not live up to one's expectations, inflexibility in human interaction, avoidance or resistance to altering one's own position even in the face of new facts, fearfulness or avoidance of confronting problems directly, a tendency to vacillate around or withdraw from conflict, and timidity, in which the individual maintains a submissive, passive demeanor in interpersonal contacts.

Some of the character traits that predict success in varied interpersonal contacts include confidence in social interactions; a preference for taking the lead in things instead of having others "make the call"; a competitive nature, with a "refuse-to-lose" attitude; a reciprocal, team-oriented approach to competition; and comfort expressing one's views, with the flexibility to adapt those views subsequent to getting new information.

Stability

While most would take it for granted that police officers should be stable and poised in their demeanor and actions no matter what conditions they encounter, it is no small feat to maintain self-control in unpredictable, possibly high-threat encounters, confusing conditions with inadequate or incomplete information, or "ambush" situations.

When an individual encounters unanticipated, rapidly changing, or chaotic conditions, his or her brain automatically undergoes a series of instinctive, survival-oriented physiological responses that include activation of the parts of the brain that create emotions and "emergency" reactions. Unless the individual is mentally prepared for a complex or dangerous interaction, he or she is much more likely to engage in an emotional, under-controlled reflex reaction than a pre-planned, proactive, rational action. Think, for example, about times in your life when, in the heat of the moment, you said or did something you immediately regretted.

A potential police officer or deputy sheriff must have demonstrated self-discipline and control in his or her actions. The individual should be able to show evidence of stability in his or her management of finances, driving behaviors, occupational history, and coping with pressures and stresses in the course of living. He or she should be consistent in mood and emotion, even under conditions or during periods of heightened pressure or stress.

The term "ego" is often used to describe how someone prioritizes the satisfaction of his or her own needs before others', as in "Boy, has he got a big ego! Look at how self-centered he is." In technical terms, however, the words **ego strength** refer to internal resources that a person uses to mediate or control how he or she discharges internal impulses and emotions. These resources are sometimes referred to as "being adult" in how one handles problems—for example, postponing immediate self-gratification and saving money in order to purchase a desired object rather than "snatching it," or remaining patient in a debate to permit people to "cool off" and lessen their defensiveness against each other.

The emotional signals of likely problems in the use of control, the management of aggression, or "badge-heavy" actions by police personnel are repeated episodes of impulsive behaviors (e.g., purchasing something on the spur of the moment on credit, lacking the necessary money) or irritated or angry reactions, whether verbal or physical. The "short-fused," easily irritated person who admits, "Yes, I do have a bit of a temper, but I never get physical," will be a prime candidate for subsequent difficulties as a law enforcement officer, because such reaction tendencies are, in and of themselves, signals of an emotional instability that could affect his or her conduct.

Conversely, an individual who is particularly uncomfortable with expressions of anger may have developed a tendency toward a timid or submissive manner as a means of avoiding interpersonal conflicts. This individual as well would be likely to have difficulty assuming a commanding presence or acting to contain a potentially assaultive, "street-wise" person.

An issue of major importance in contemporary law enforcement is how police officers and sheriff deputies manage, mediate, and control aggression. Indeed, most of the scandals that have rocked law enforcement have involved the police using some form of force against others. If I were to provide a report on an applicant for police work that included the comment "This is an aggressive person," a police executive would likely look askance at the applicant and avoid hiring him or her.

The word "aggressive," when used to describe a police officer, often conjures up images in people's minds of actions that are excessive, wrong, or unprofessional. However, in truth, aggressive action is required at times to save the life of victims of crime. Aggression is not a dirty word. It is the very essence of mastery over obstacles. If aggression on the part of officers is minimized in their training and policies, then perpetrators of crime will have a much greater degree of initiative and power to hurt others. This does a disservice to society.

Take for example the currently controversial issue of vehicle pursuits of fleeing suspects by police officers following the commission of a violent crime—e.g., the murder of a police officer, a bank robbery, or a carjacking. It has been debated whether police officers should be made to cease their pursuit of fleeing felons to avoid the possibility of innocent persons being accidentally hurt or killed.

If permitted, the fleeing felon will continue victimizing others, because that is what criminals do. Whose mother, husband, wife, or child will be the next victim of a criminal who could have been stopped with aggressive and relentless police action? Society must come to understand that the price they will pay for a more passive police officer is a more aggressive criminal. As Dr. Samenow points out in his study of criminal psychology, the criminal mind is such that the criminal continues to plan and initiate crimes until his actions and environment are controlled (Samenow, 1984).

A Sense of Mission

One of the major differences between those who freeze or flee from any contact with severe or lethal threat and those who rush toward the threat to combat and extinguish it is a sense of mission or purpose. A sense of mission in law enforcement refers to the willingness and motivation of an officer or deputy to suspend his or her personal comfort and safety in order to confront difficult or dangerous circumstances for the benefit of others. It applies to those officers and deputies who are totally committed to the mission of police work, who will, without thinking, stay the course in "tough times," and are willing to sacrifice their own lives to save a person they do not even know.

The mission of law enforcement is a bit more complex than a military mission. In a peaceful society, the law enforcement mission involves the police's social responsibility to create a feeling of order and safety in the community they serve. Indeed, the very definition of the word "policing" includes the officer or deputy's fundamental mission: "To govern; to control, regulate, or keep in order; to make clean and put in order; to supervise the operation, execution, or administration of, to prevent or detect and prosecute violations of rules and regulations" (Merriam-Webster Collegiate Dictionary, 2000).

Much of the difference in the quality of police officers or deputy sheriffs I have interviewed or treated in therapy over the past twenty years can be explained by the possession or lack of a feeling of obligation and responsibility to serve and protect others, versus the desire to enhance their personal position or gain.

An extremely important component of the sense of mission is a promise made among those who serve when they pin on the badge: "If you need me, I will be there. I will risk my own well-being, even sacrifice my life, to get to you. I will forsake the comfort of my home and family to save you—for we are partners." Such is the bond that used to exist in the police family. Inability to keep that promise in more recent times has caused officers and their families great suffering.

The traditional police attitudes and practices that existed until 1992 (the year in which Los Angeles police officers were videotaped striking Rodney King) were feared and mistrusted by many members of the public. But one common feature in police officers up to that time—less common today—was that sense of mission that is crucial in determining what risks a police officer takes. When I say that this sense of mission is less common today, I do not mean that there are not daily occurrences of excellent, selfless police work occurring across the country. Rather, the point made here is that the injuries suffered by both society and police have resulted in a defensive and somewhat less active posture by a disturbingly large number of contemporary police officers.

An officer's sense of mission may be damaged in a defensive response to the external societal and organizational environment the officer encounters—including the public perceptions that are communicated to police officers when they become involved in a politically sensitive police action. One of the consequences of a "broad-brushed" painting of police officers as the "bad guys" when distressing events occur is a pressure exerted upon officers to become more pragmatic and self-protective—instead of mission-oriented.

I interviewed a number of veterans of law enforcement for this book to ensure that I provided credible and accurate information. I selected each officer because of his or her demonstrated expertise and excellence. These officers' common perspective regarding their experiences over the many years of their combined performance of police work was that they lived with a passion for their work. It was a calling to them. They believed that they were "meant" to do police work and had been placed there by God to serve others. When I asked them how they defined their mission as police officers and deputy sheriffs, they communicated the calling to do what no one else can do—to go to places that others were fleeing from to save the innocent.

These interviews occurred prior to September 11, 2001. What the New York City police officers and firefighters did in charging up scores of flights of stairs in the World Trade Center buildings was their mission. They knew of no other way to live. Their sacrifice, and the feeling of mission of the heroes who continue to live and serve, is the truest definition of honor I have observed in almost sixty years of being alive.

To make candidates into such police officers and deputy sheriffs today, law enforcement institutions are facing a substantial challenge. First, within the past ten to fifteen years, the generational characteristics of the applicant pool that police work has drawn from have been, on the whole, quite different from those in preceding years.

Many of today's youth were raised either by single parents who worked or in two-parent homes where both parents worked. While this is certainly not an indictment of working parents, the fact remains that many of today's applicant pool for police work had a different developmental experience than the generation whose family life was idealized in such television shows as *Father Knows Best* and *Ozzie and Harriet*.

Today's entering police officers may respond with a greater degree of familiarity to a computer monitor than to interpersonal conflict resolution with someone of a different ethnicity, and see themselves more as individual achievers than as members of a collective pursuit. In addition, the roles that those who serve in law enforcement are asked to play, and the methods by which police officers are educated, trained, and socialized, are changing without any "how-to" manual to guide those whose job it is to prepare the next generation of police officers and deputy sheriffs needed to protect and serve.

4. Shaping the New Police Recruit

The breadth and variety of work activities expected of police officers and deputy sheriffs are enormous, requiring the coordinated acts of an entire police organization all the time and in all circumstances encountered in the community—not an easy task. Regardless of the challenges posed by the size of their task, the background of the recruits, and the political environment, every police agency still must educate and train new members in such a manner that they fulfill the responsibilities given to law enforcement.

There is an ongoing turnover in police personnel, as one generation retires and another begins. While television shows popularize police work and allow police officers to show that they are human, it is rarely made public that a substantial number, at times a majority, of officers and deputies do not reach a "normal" service retirement of twenty-five to thirty or more years on the job. Some incident, illness, injury, death, or accumulation of stressful encounters prevents the completion of their career of service (Fell, Richard, and Wallace, 1980; Violanti, Vena, and Marshall, 1986; Blum, 1998; et al.).

Police agencies must provide recruits with the skills and knowledge necessary to perform police tasks so that they may take the place of those who have left. Recruits must be introduced to the agency in a way that ensures that the particular agency's characteristics and practices will be maintained or enhanced. Therefore, the development and formation of specific attitudes and values in recruits—in addition to the skills and behaviors necessary to perform police work—must be established in all officers who work within the agencies.

It is not an easy task to "make" a good police officer. The public often is unaware that such an achievement involves substantially more than just the skill of the individual person performing police duties. While the media's attention is primarily focused on the working police officer or deputy sheriff, the factors that determine the degree of excellence or mediocrity within the police agency can mainly be observed in the characteristics and processes of the organization itself. Once a person becomes a police or deputy sheriff recruit, his or her quality of life and level of accomplishment depend upon pleasing and satisfying those in the ranks above—groups that sometimes have conflicting priorities. Further, what is "pleasing" and "satisfying" to a department's leadership depends upon what that leader's or those leaders' expectations are for what makes a "good" cop in their agency. Ideally, an agency will provide an atmosphere that nurtures the qualities necessary for good policing rather than breeding self-aggrandizement, self-protection, self-interest, disillusionment, and fear.

The most consistently powerful vehicle of socialization, regardless of the police agency or type of jurisdiction, is the Field Training Officer (FTO). It is the FTO who trains the rookie officer or deputy in how to do police work, providing the practical training that cannot be had at the Academy.

The trainee quickly learns that positive evaluations are achieved by performing tasks exactly as the FTO performs them. The demeanor, body language, tone, attitude, and verbal behavior used by the FTO in, for instance, car stops, domestic disturbances, report calls, "pat downs," warrant checks, and arrests will be internalized by the trainee. The modeled behaviors and attitudes become the trainee's own behaviors and attitudes. They also become the conditioned responses the trainee will likely use throughout his or her career. Hence, the experience and communication skills of those staffing FTO assignments are of critical importance. Unfortunately, staffing problems, budgetary constraints, and court orders have often resulted in officers with only two to three years of experience providing Field Training to entering recruits. Any poor habits developed at this stage caused by inexperienced trainers will remain with police officers for the rest of their careers.

Social Values vs. Tactics
The largest percentage of policing work-time is actually taken up with numerous responsibilities other than law enforcement and crime fighting. Recruits must therefore develop an interactive, interpersonal, collaborative, and service-oriented demeanor to fulfill non-law-enforcement duties. The majority of police contacts today involve maintenance of community order or civil- and assistance-related activities. These activities are characterized by a more or less equal relationship between officer or deputy and citizen, because these circumstances are civil in nature and do not fall within law enforcement's areas of authority. A value system in which the officer and the public are equal partners in their interactions is inherent in community policing, in contrast to traditional incident-driven policing, in which the officer must immediately take control of the situation. In community policing, the police and the community are separated only by their differing tasks, and no longer engage in a vertical relationship defined by the officer's authority over the public.

But police officers must also be trained at the Academy in the tactics and demeanor they will need to stay alive in street encounters, especially in the area of self-confidence and assertion. Recruits are trained that as officers or deputies they should keep themselves in a position to remain in control at all times. Control enables an officer or deputy to overcome any and all situations he or she encounters. The message is clear—take command, *be absolutely certain of that command*, and you will be victorious. The very survival of the officer requires the maintenance of this control. This is emphasized over and over again from the first day of Academy training. Its implementation requires a specific character: one should be assertive, immovable, at times aggressive and competitive; maintain a "refuse to lose" attitude; and possess the drive to seize the initiative and maintain it no matter what one is faced with. In this way, the will of the law is imposed upon the law violator.

The need for command presence in policing is based much less upon the social values applied in community policing, and much more in the science of tactics. Police tactics are developed empirically from lessons learned in the field, especially when police officers have been murdered or thwarted in carrying out their duties (Wemmer, 1999; 2000). Well-meaning attempts to insert social values into policing may, if imposed upon policies that determine the rules of engagement, easily result in officers being preoccupied or distracted by having to consider a subject's feelings even when that subject's actions pose a threat to someone's safety. Hesitancy, delay, or a startled reaction in police actions during a high-threat encounter will activate an officer's instinctive human biological defenses and cause him or her to violate the principles he or she was taught about tactical responses. These are the incidents that result in negative scrutiny of one kind or another. These are also the times when police officers are murdered (California Commission on Police Standards and Training, 1996; Federal Bureau of Investigation, 1992). Training in tactics and critical decision making under stress is crucial in keeping such incidents to a minimum, as the following story will illustrate.

He was a political extremist who lived in a converted military armored personnel carrier from the 1930s. The vehicle was modified with a windmill generator, a patio enclosure on the roof, and an escape hatch into the body of the vehicle. There were portholes on three sides of the vehicle, and the fourth contained a bulletproof windshield. This man had been contacted previously by the United States Secret Service for threats he had made against the President.

For reasons that are still unknown, the man went one day to the motor home in the next stall and shot his neighbor over forty times with a shotgun and .30-.30 assault rifle. He then strode down the aisle toward the mobile home used as a residence for the 24-hour security guards who were assigned to the storage yard. Circling all four sides of the unit, he fired shot after shot into the mobile home. Inside, the father and his teenage son hit the floor and dialed 911.

The police helicopter was the first to arrive, equipped with a forward-looking infrared radar (FLIR). The helicopter crew discovered the shooter's position and notified incoming patrol officers that the suspect was walking back toward his armored motor home. Arriving officers attempted to rescue the man and his son in the embattled motor home and were fired upon by the suspect, who was now on top of his fortified vehicle with a direct line of fire to the police and to the guard's motor home. The officers were forced under fire to crawl underneath boats, motor homes, and other recreational vehicles stored in the yard to escape the hail of high-caliber gunfire.

When people need help, they call 911 for the police. When the police need help, they call for the Special Weapons and Tactics Team (SWAT Team). SWAT Teams are trained constantly and are equipped with the firepower needed to control events that only rarely happen, but are of a severe, life-threatening, catastrophic nature.

Because of the exigent conditions they were faced with, the members of the local SWAT Team were immediately deployed without first being able to scout and determine the best position. As one of the sniper teams was climbing onto a roof, with one of the officers covering the suspect as his partner was attempting to reach the top, the suspect fired on them. The cover officer immediately returned fire. The immediacy of his armed response caused the suspect's bullets to miss the climbing officer by just two inches. It was later learned that the cover officer's return fire had also grazed the suspect and forced him to withdraw into his fortified vehicle.

Four snipers were now deployed, as two tactical teams established an inner perimeter around the fortified vehicle. The police quickly discovered that negotiation was not an option. This suspect returned a barrage of fire with every attempt made to gain his surrender.

One team attempted to fire tear gas through the windshield, but the 12-gauge slugs could not penetrate. Rifle slugs were fired that only served to crack the windshield. The suspect fired through the portholes each time the tactical team tried to deploy gas.

The suspect would emerge onto the patio enclosure with his clothes off and his hands raised as he looked around, attempting to identify the positions of the tactical teams. He then returned to the vehicle before the police could reach him.

Jackie held one of the advance positions. When the team was deployed, he had been at the point as they carefully advanced towards the armored vehicle. Now Jackie's gas team made another attempt to penetrate the fortress with a .37-mm gas projectile. The suspect was waiting for them. He jumped from the hatch onto the enclosed patio roof and began to fire. "I was getting rained on by shotgun pellets," Jackie told me. "He had me pinned in a corner. I thought I was going to die and never see my boys or wife again."

The rules of engagement that had been given to the snipers and the tactical teams had been a "yellow light." That meant that they could fire upon the suspect only to defend themselves or others. No other authorization to fire had been given to the snipers when they simultaneously saw the suspect appear on the top of his vehicle and take dead aim on Jackie trapped below. One shot was heard. The suspect's head appeared to Jackie to just go into pieces as the shooter fell down, lifeless.

The sergeant collected all the snipers and began the investigative process by asking them who had fired the shot. Three of the four snipers raised their hands. The sergeant smiled at them as he said, "Nice try, guys, but only one shot was fired." He asked again, and again each sniper acknowledged his decision to shoot the suspect in order to save the lives of the embattled officers. It was later discovered that the suspect had been struck simultaneously by three police rounds from three independent tactical decisions made and acted upon at a distance of over seventy-five yards. They were proud, not because they had taken someone's life, but because they had done their job well, and innocent people had been saved. Decisive police action was required in this dangerous incident, and saved lives that would otherwise have been lost.

The snipers were not traumatized by their use of lethal force. They had clearly observed the danger to innocent people. Each had individually seen the exigency of firing, because Jackie and the rest of the gas team had been directly in the suspect's line of fire. However, one of them, a veteran of many years of police work, held his hands out to me and facetiously complained, "Doc, this is the Friday of my duty week," a reference to the fact that he would not get the extra three days of time off work that officers involved in fatal shootings are given by his department, because his weekend fell on the same days.

Those who saw either the live coverage or a tape of the North Hollywood Bank Robbery in 1997 learned quickly the amount of damage and terror that just two men protected by full-body armor and spraying the neighborhood with automatic weapon fire could immediately produce. The police officers who contained these two dangerous persons were armed with the training and preparation required to save the lives of the innocent. Any police officer who lacks such proficiency in unanticipated high-risk conditions—not because of any deficiency in officer ability, but due to a lack of continuing training and practice under adversity—will be placed at a disadvantage that should be unacceptable to us.

Obstacles to Training
Early training experiences need to teach officers safety and survival procedures and the tactical actions that are required to place them in

positions of advantage when they encounter danger. The officer or deputy's survival in tactical encounters will depend upon his or her reacting immediately, without the need for conscious thought or decision at the moment of crisis. It takes too much time to consider whether an officer's approach to a subject is considerate of the subject's feelings when that subject is raising a gun or knife and pointing it at the officer. The combination of formal education and on-the-job training is supposed to create an officer who will react automatically, decisively, and with the demeanor of command.

The principles and practices of community policing that were introduced into the Academy curriculum a few years ago constitute another, diverse set of skills for recruits to master, with a repertoire of actions other than arrest and patrol procedures, safety, and tactics. Today's trainees must also learn procedures involving collaboration, networking, and resource acquisition, to be used in solving community problems via a partnership and collegial relationship with community members.

Recruits are now being expected to learn more than ever before. Yet academies are often of shorter duration than those of the past, due to cost containment efforts by states, counties, and municipalities. Fiscal limits imposed by the Board of Supervisors of a large, urban sheriff's department, for example, have resulted in the Sheriff's Academy being shortened from twenty-four to eighteen weeks in duration. The same penal codes, rules, laws, police procedures, and skills that were taught in twenty-four weeks are still required by the State Commission on Police Standards and Training (the state governing authority regarding the standards that must be met to perform police work).

Therefore, the amount of knowledge that can be provided to new recruits may be reduced. The ability to apply learned skills is likely to be reduced as well, because a truncated learning experience will have to be based more upon skill-building only, rather than upon a broader degree of knowledge about what each skill means and how it fits into the repertoire of police tools. In other words, recruits are trained in methods without learning the theory behind the method that would permit it to be properly applied in a wider range of conditions without delay. A recruit will have the time to learn arrest-and-control techniques and procedures, but may not have the time to integrate these tools into a mental model of tactical strategy that can be immediately and appropriately applied to unanticipated, often confusing conditions—an extremely dangerous deficit in their education.

The benefit of possessing internal mental models of police tactics and applying the tools therein to current events is that one does not have to keep "re-inventing the wheel" each time one is required to act. Once someone has learned a mental model of how to ride a bicycle, for example, he or she "just does it" without needing to think about the complex process of pedaling and balance. When police officers do not possess a shared mental model that provides the foundation for the range of tactical responses available to them, there is a greater likelihood of some type of error in their response. This is so because it just takes too much time for police officers to react to emergent situations if they have to delay their response in order to figure out what to do. Their response must be automatic, or people will die unnecessarily. This is the reason why I believe that "procedure only" teaching is insufficient to adequately prepare police officers for contemporary encounters.

In addition, the majority of Police Academies have now suspended many if not all of the activities that involved the introduction of adversity, pressure, and stressful conditions into the learning process. In the past, Academies were militaristic in their drill and in the creation of adversity in the training process. Now an adult education model is used, partly because decision makers believe that this model will produce officers who feel more of a sense of partnership with the community they serve, and feel less like an "occupying army." Another reason for the change is that policy makers believed that people learn better when they are not "stressed out" (Lim, 2001).

71

But, because they are permitted to avoid immediate risk and adversity, police trainees and recruits may be receiving an educational experience that could result in their being deficient in the control and management of high-risk, adverse, chaotic, and disordered conditions in the field.

When an individual officer encounters a crisis situation, like any human being, his or her reaction time consists of the time it takes to assess what the problem is and appraise its level of threat or severity, the time it takes to make a decision to act, and the time that action takes to be performed. While many people can adjust to situations that are predictable and stable over time, very few can, on a continual and predictable basis, react immediately to totally unanticipated, rapidly changing, or chaotic conditions without some degradation in their mental concentration and focus of attention, their ability to make effective judgments, their poise, and their self-control. For example, most people, when startled or acutely frightened by something, will spend a moment or more in a state of shock, not doing much in the way of analytical thinking or purposeful actions. They cannot immediately **act upon** the situation, but must first **react to** it.

This moment of uncertainty or lack of consciousness often creates a phenomenon referred to as a **perceptual lag**. For a police officer or deputy, the perceptual lag is the time it takes to re-orient his or her mind to a new, unplanned-for circumstance. It is within these moments that too many police officers have been killed, or have engaged in acts that will haunt them for the rest of their lives. They had not been trained to prevent such a momentary shock reaction, even though there is now technology available to do so (see for example Blum, 2000; Cannon-Bowers and Salas, 1998).

It is true indeed that the amount of time police spend in order maintenance and service-oriented activities is far more than the time spent in tactical encounters. However, it is spurious logic to think that police personnel should therefore be trained any less in the ability to successfully and purposefully encounter "split-second" circumstances that could well determine life or death for themselves and others.

In general, police officers do not now possess viable training and preparation to engage in critical decision making under stressful conditions. They are well trained in what to do and how to do it, but not in how to manage and control their concentration, perceptions, judgment, thinking, and decision making when chaos is occurring or when they are ambushed. Society has taken for granted that police officers possess this skill. It has been my experience, however, that, while some officers are extremely skilled at making decisions under stress, just as many officers have difficulty doing so. Without this critical skill, a large number of officers, when they encounter rapidly changing conditions, unanticipated or unknown circumstances, or chaos, will be more prone to the kinds of errors that have created such a furor in society.

Another difficulty facing today's police recruits and their teachers is that most of the applicant pool now seeking to enter police work has less experience with adjusting to changing social conditions than recruits of the past. **Social adjustment** refers to the recognition, via social and interpersonal cues, of how one needs to adapt one's demeanor, behavior, and actions to successfully meet the requirements of changing social or interpersonal conditions—and the ability to act appropriately upon that recognition. If an individual runs into severe difficulty with a computer or game, he or she can press the "escape" or "new game" key and get another opportunity to succeed. Today's young applicant appears highly skilled at reasoning and solving dilemmas and problems when the conditions of the problem are stable and predictable and the tempo of change can be controlled. The contemporary applicant appears to have somewhat more difficulty with rapidly changing, unanticipated, or chaotic conditions.

What this means is that these recruits will make very good police officers if they are provided a mentoring experience that facilitates their development of critical decision-making skills under adverse conditions. They will be less effective if they are left with procedural skill but not skill in deciding what, when, how, and how much of a tactical response is needed when they have encountered a previously unknown condition.

Critical Decision-Making Skills

I believe that the single most important skill for a police officer or deputy sheriff to possess is the ability to engage in critical decision making under adverse conditions. Given that being able to think decisively and quickly in high-stress situations is a characteristic of successful conflict resolution, one would think that teaching decision making would be of primary importance in the early education of police recruits. Because of the required learning areas that the state certifying agency demands, academies very often do not expend enough time ensuring that each trainee is qualified in critical decision making under stressful conditions. Agencies are often left with only the hope that their new police officers or deputy sheriffs possess this skill as an inherent character trait.

In a curriculum devoted to critical thinking skills, an individual would be provided with the knowledge needed to develop an internal mental model of how things "fit together." Once a theory or mental model existed in the mind, the individual could much more easily integrate a current condition or task with methods learned from a retrievable body of knowledge, experience, or science. Then, given sufficient practice at using the methods, and the ability to accurately recognize what situation is being encountered, the officer or deputy would have a learning base to enable him or her to manage a much greater variety of police contacts correctly.

Without a knowledge base sufficient for new recruits to develop mental models of how the content that they are learning fits into actual police performance, officers and deputies will be unable to automatically retrieve previous learning once a condition is recognized. They will be forced instead to consider and think through what to do in each given type of event each and every time.

This will place the officer or deputy at a distinct disadvantage, because an individual's reaction time is much faster when the action being performed requires no concentration or thought.

I am not going to present case studies of officers and deputies whose deaths I have studied over the twenty years of my career. Nor is it my place to second-guess the tactical decisions of police officers. As I have said elsewhere, I certainly lay no claim to being an expert in the science of police tactics. In the past twenty years, however, I have stood over the graves of twenty-three murdered law enforcement officers, and have worked to assist many more officers and their families when they have been injured by a felon's assault. I cannot agree with any strategy of education, training, hiring, or promotion that lessens the degree to which a police officer is capable of engaging in immediate critical thinking and decision making under stressful conditions, because it is the mental activity of the officer that will decide the difference between life and death. Law enforcement continues to "look with a blind eye" at the importance of this kind of training.

Experts in the field of police tactics and officer safety have collected a tremendous amount of information regarding successful assaults against police officers. They have continually seen the need to train officers' minds to make tactical decisions from this body of knowledge. They know that in the best of circumstances, officers see a vision of tactical options from which they select the solution most likely to increase the probability of success and survival (Wemmer, 1999; Osuna, 2000; Deuel, 2001; Miller, 2002).

The experts have studied suspect behaviors prior to and during assaults against police officers. They know that it is critical for the officer to "read the scene," to watch what is unusual about a person's actions and ascertain what the suspect's reaction to the officer's presence is. Is he compliant? Is there danger? Has this individual committed a crime? What does the officer have to contend with? How can the officer act to increase safety? How quickly does the officer need to act?

These experts have felt concern that officers appear to have the tendency to rush in, walk forward, and approach the suspect—to make something happen. They have found that there are many incidents in which a suspect has deceived the officer and that, by rushing in, the officer has not used all the resources that could have been applied to that set of circumstances (Wemmer, 1999; Deuel, 2001). In still other cases, they found out that officers had delayed or hesitated in their application of police tactics, thereby allowing the suspect to gain the initiative and control of the conflict.

There is clearly a body of knowledge that is empirical and replicable sufficient to develop expert levels of competence in the science of tactics and work fitness (to be discussed in detail below). Self-control of the mind, and expertise in critical thinking under pressure, are the best possible protections against improper police actions. The skills and knowledge available with such expertise can then be retrieved and applied properly and rapidly over a wide range of diverse encounters without performance being degraded by ambush, chaos, or rapid change from the outside, and/or the intrusive influence of instinctive, as opposed to purposeful, police responses during "the heat of the moment."

While it is laudable for police policies to prohibit and control the likelihood of officer misapplication of rules or misconduct, such policies should never be permitted to minimize the role of discretionary critical thinking by police officers. Officers in the field have to make decisions under critical, adverse, or stressful conditions and must generate and implement the proper strategy to apply to each and every circumstance under conditions of severe time compression. Critical thinking and decision-making skills should be the goal of law enforcement alongside efforts to ensure integrity and ethics in the delivery of police services.

Tactical Plans in Officer Problem-Solving Tasks
Tactical planning is the method that is most often taught to recruits to enable them to overcome obstacles they may encounter in the

course of their duties in a safe and appropriate manner. Tactical planning saves lives and identifies proper actions for officers who won't have the time to stop to consider what to do during a high-risk encounter. In traditional tactical planning, the officer develops a series of hypothetical scenarios he or she might encounter during a regular tour of duty. The officer then thinks through the range of possible reactions and/or responses that would be appropriate to any given circumstance—such as cover, concealment, and other actions that would place him or her in an advantageous position.

The purpose of planning is to ensure that the officer is able to use proactive methods of command. Being proactive gives the officer the tactical edge, or initiative, needed to avoid being overwhelmed or surprised by the acts of the subject and thereby forced into a reactive, disadvantageous position. Being proactive in an encounter permits the officer to control the most unpredictable, unusual, or disturbing subjects by taking the initiative away from the subject and thus gaining the ability to direct how the situation ends.

To be proactive, however, officers must be accurate in their assessment of the scene and subject. They cannot be proactive if they encounter a situation that differs from their prediction or their personal habits of police work and thus requires them to spend time correcting their assessment and switching to a different tactical response than they had planned. The initiative that they possess is then lessened by the time it takes for them to change course and react. Officers must continually be supervised and trained (i.e., reminded) to avoid any mind-set (e.g., being complacent) that would compromise how they approach an incident. Such important training and supervision in proper mind-set and activities that ensure proper mental conditioning are rarely, if ever, performed.

This is certainly not to say that use of adult education as well as prior experience with learned procedures is totally improper for police training efforts. Prior experiences are invaluable and necessary in most of the situations that officers will encounter in the field. However, other aids to officers in the process of determining the proper tactics to use in the here-and-now may be crucial in some situations when all the past experience an officer has had cannot be readily applied to the new incident.

In 1986, Marvin Cohen and colleagues performed research for the military in the aftermath of incidents involving the USS Stark and USS Vincennes. They developed a method that proved relevant and useful for application to training personnel to maintain their concentration, judgment, and effective decision making during novel and disordered events. The training method is designed to enhance individuals' use of prior knowledge, enabling them to apply this knowledge purposefully and consciously to help them make decisions in chaotic conditions (Cohen, in Cannon-Bowers and Salas, 1998).

The first stage of training in this method of decision making under stress teaches the trainees about the **identification of information-conclusion relationships** within the evolving encounter. This means that there is an articulated awareness developed in trainees that as officers they will make, based on the information they first observe at the scene, an initial set of assumptions (or "argument") regarding the condition of the scene they have encountered and the subject's apparent reaction to their presence. The first stage essentially involves making inferences about the intent of the subject and others within the scene. This has to be a learned process, because under normal circumstances, police officers are not likely to be conscious of the fact that they are establishing inferences about what conditions they are about to encounter as they enter a scene. They tend to receive the information automatically, without a specific concentration or awareness that they are doing so.

The second stage of decision making is **critiquing**, a process used to identify problems in the arguments that support a conclusion (e.g., whether or not a subject demonstrates a hostile intent, or which disputant in a chaotic conflict is the victim) pertaining to the situation the officer has encountered. Critiquing can result in the discovery of three kinds of flaws in an argument: **incompleteness**, **conflict**, and **unreliability** (Cannon-Bowers and Salas, 1998).

An argument is **incomplete** if it provides insufficient information to support a decision. (For example, the subject's behavior may suggest the existence of a mental disorder, but this says nothing about his intent). Two arguments **conflict** with one another if they provide support both for and against a conclusion, respectively. (For example, the subject's demeanor and words suggest a hostile intent, while his slow and passive behaviors argue for a less threatening encounter). Finally, an argument is **unreliable** if the support it provides for a conclusion depends on unexamined assumptions, e.g., an officer's pre-judgment of the situation.

The third stage in decision making will activate decisions that have the effect of **correcting** the circumstances that the officer perceived as a problem. Correcting steps may instigate external action, such as the act of placing the suspect in custody; or the officer may decide to collect additional data.

In the latter case, the officer will perform mental actions that regulate the operation of the **recognitional system** of the brain. These actions include purposefully shifting the focus of his or her attention and concentration to identify the actual, highest-priority elements of the scene he or she must manage; and, if necessary, revising prior assumptions that have proved false. Purposefully prioritizing one's reactions also results in the activation of the part of the brain that automatically retrieves all past learning from memory and facilitates the bringing of additional, currently available knowledge into view for the purpose of judgment and decision.

The rate at which the officer decides to intervene is of major importance to his or her success. In some instances, patience and a slowing of the rate of police action are required. This is often the case, for example, when a police officer contacts a person who appears mentally disordered. Other incidents might require the officer to engage in actions that disrupt, control, or contain an individual whose actions present a threat. There are three primary rates or time orientations that police officers can apply; these are termed **proactive**, **predictive**, and **reactive**.

Proactive time orientation provides the maximum amount of initiative. It is most often present at low levels of threat—when the purpose of the officer's action is to influence the intent or limit the options of a possibly dangerous but not yet assaultive person. Verbal interactions intended to produce a calming effect are one example of a police response from a proactive orientation.

Predictive time orientation is most often present at moderate levels of threat, when a person's probable actions are predicted by his behaviors. For example, during a domestic disturbance, one individual may threaten to assault another while pointing a finger or waving an arm in a threatening manner, hitting a wall. The officer may respond in a predictive time orientation with actions designed to disrupt or defeat the suspect's planned action; exploit a position of advantage over the suspect; avoid a position of disadvantage; and marshal the resources he or she will need to accomplish control. Verbal tools may not be viable in predictive conditions, as the subject's actions could well require physical containment due to heightened emotions or other factors.

The **reactive** time orientation represents the least amount of initiative. It occurs when the subject's action (such as a surprise assault against the officer or another person) is underway and the officer seeks to limit the damage. Verbal tools are not viable in these conditions. Unfortunately, research has documented a number of cases of officers continuing to give verbal commands to a suspect who was in the act of attempting to murder them (California Commission on Police Officer Standards and Training, 1996).

These time orientations overlap each other in practice during the training process. Their application in the field requires assessment of the characteristics of the person and situation the officer has encountered, and how viable one strategy or another will likely prove for this circumstance.

Successful officers will develop flexible, adaptive problem-solving methods that they can use to determine the proper course of action. They will not depend rigidly upon procedures that may have worked for them in the past. They will maintain their presence of mind and continue to use accurate information provided by their senses regardless of the level of chaos surrounding them.

In other words, since the nature of the police response depends upon the situational characteristics of the incident, the officer must be able to apply methods that he or she has learned, and to select those methods based upon a conceptual understanding of human behavior, the science of tactics, the response tendencies of previously encountered criminals, and the best application of strategies in the here-and-now for the proper police response.

Implications for Police Training in Tactics

There is an underlying expectation implicit in efforts to teach tactical skills to police officers. The need for the maximal performance of the procedure or skill is an unstated expectation in all police training efforts so that the officer gains mastery in the actual field encounter. Control of difficult scenes involves a simple but critical task on the part of the officer. He or she must gain and maintain the initiative and control in any encounter, or else the subject will possess them instead, and the officer will be forced to react to, rather than determine, the outcome. Gaining control and initiative can alleviate the problematic fact that police officers invariably begin their attempts to control a scene somewhat behind the subject's actions.

Gaining the advantage requires the officer to achieve mastery of the encounter under conditions of ambiguous, inconsistent, and/or confusing information and actions. It means that the officer rapidly and accurately perceives the tactical requirements of the scene and engages in decisive action with the proper time orientation to overcome the inertia brought about by the subject's actions.

In order to gain initiative and control, officers must develop habitual patterns of rapid and decisive action. A critical part of

81

tactical training is inculcating a sense of urgency so that no delay from prior values, expectations, indecision, hesitancy, or personal concerns places the officer further behind the subject's actions.

The officer must also be able to respond with patience when it is called for. The consequence of the officer's falling behind or acting too quickly will be a greater risk of inappropriate tactical reactions, often prompting officers to use greater levels of force than otherwise would have been required.

It is relatively simple to teach an officer how to perform a task in a classroom setting. A class has a syllabus and plan; specific content is presented and the parameters of the task are well defined. The students and instructor are able to predict the type of encounter that will be used for training purposes, and can prepare for certification tests by using the class curriculum.

The management of a police encounter in the field, however, will not occur with the same stable pattern or predictability and controlled tempo found in the classroom. Proficiency in managing rapidly changing, chaotic, or unanticipated incidents will require that officers develop **adaptive expertise**. This skill permits the individual to recognize changes in task priorities and conditions, and to shift the tactical response accordingly (Kozlowski, 1998).

It obviously does not make sense for an officer confronted with a lethal threat to take the time to stop and engage in conscious analysis ("Now let me see . . . they're drawing a gun, they're pointing it at me . . . I see a muzzle, I am in grave danger, am I justified to use lethal force due to a fear for my life?"). Such mental activity will obviously result in a hesitation that places the officer and witnesses or victims in grave danger. On the other hand, the vast majority of police contacts do not result in police officers experiencing lethal threat against them, or other conditions that would require the use of lethal force.

Officers must, of course, protect the civil rights and lives of citizens by using the least severe and intrusive control measures in the performance of their duties. Their actions must be driven by strong moral and ethical values that prohibit them from impropriety under the color of their authority. They must not allow personal preference or political ideology to influence their actions as officers, but must be controlled by a system of public protection through policy, law, and constitutional safeguards. If the police are to abide by the above mission for their comportment, they must take some amount of time to properly assess whether the conditions at a given scene give them probable cause to act.

Research reported in the *Wound Ballistics Review* (Tobin and Fackler, 2001) studied how long it took for a police officer to fire his or her handgun when presented with two scenarios of varying complexity. The time from the appearance of the scenario until the shot was fired included the time needed for the officer to perceive the threat and decide to fire (decision time) and the time it took to fire his or her weapon (reaction-response). The researchers' conclusions verified that the time necessary for officers to perceive a threat and decide to fire their handgun increases with the complexity of the threat. They reported that the mean, or average, decision time and reaction-response time for police officers was approximately 0.5 seconds for each, comprising a total of one second.

In one scenario, a man with a shotgun stepped out from behind a car door and pointed the shotgun at the officer in a threatening manner. The second, more complex scenario depicted an assassination attempt that took place in the hallway of a busy courthouse, where there were several people present in the hall to distract the officer. The average time it took officers to make the decision to use lethal force in the simple scenario was 0.211 seconds. In the more complex scenario, the average time it took officers to make that decision was 0.895 seconds, over half a second longer—a period of time in which several shots may be fired by a suspect.

Undoubtedly, rapidly changing conditions, distracting conditions, unanticipated threats, and/or chaotic levels of stimuli complicate the officer's ability to make accurate assessments and decisions. Officer-involved shootings most often contain elements that distract and/or complicate the officer's decision process. It is probable that some officer-involved shootings have occurred as an instinctive survival reaction (at times referred to as a **startle reaction**) by the individual officer in fear of his or her life, rather than as a result of analysis and judgment.

Those who are quickest to make accurate decisions that are based upon moral and ethical values, compliance with policy and law, and the proper application of tactics, and those who have practiced and trained and prepared themselves sufficiently for this one single moment in time, will tend to be the ones who return home to their families after their duty watch has ended. In addition, officers who accurately assess the severity and imminence of threats (e.g., from a mentally disordered person) will be less likely to fall behind the subject's actions, and therefore less likely to feel the need to use greater degrees of force. Where such skill or conditioning is absent, grave consequences may ensue.

In just a single two-week period in 2002, for example, police officers from a large, urban southern California police department were involved in two fatal shootings of mentally disordered persons, one of whom was brandishing a large stone, and one who was swinging a shopping cart at officers (*Los Angeles Times*, July 2, 2002). The district attorney in their county found that the officers had acted properly, as they had been reasonably in fear of their lives and the lives of witnesses. The shootings did, however, rekindle controversies regarding the amount and quality of training police officers receive in dealing with mentally disordered persons.

In the late 1960s to early 1970s the process of de-institutionalization of the mentally ill and disordered began in earnest as a primary feature of the Community Mental Health movement. The theory was that these individuals, instead of being "warehoused" in large, impersonal facilities, would be much more functional and "better off" in community-based residential treatment facilities and group homes. Unfortunately, most of these community-based resources ended up closing down, or failed to materialize. The result is a large population of persons whose actions, speech, demeanor, and thought processes appear foreign and disturbing to mainstream society, of which police officers are members. Officers have often been unable to understand and effectively communicate with such individuals, who comprise a goodly portion of police-citizen contacts. The consequence has been that police officers' efforts to resolve contacts with mentally disordered persons have been criticized as unnecessarily violent.

To my dismay, none of the recent complaints regarding police officer uses of lethal force during contact with mentally disordered persons referred to the need to ensure that police officers are not only more knowledgeable, familiar, and skilled with mentally ill persons, but also expert in making decisions under stress.

The fact remains that many police officers today are just not psychologically prepared or predisposed to put a resistant or threatening suspect down immediately through the application of physical force. Too many police officers permit fear of punishment, or their perception of themselves as providers of community service as opposed to crime fighters, to limit their use of aggression when responding to a threatening suspect or subject. The continuing expectation and/or fear of punishment for using force and/or aggressive action will result in a conditioned response in the brain. Officers will then be prone to develop an "automatic" or reflex (subliminal as opposed to conscious) association between the immediate and decisive application of an aggressive response to a threatening person, and an expectation that negative consequences will befall them for doing their job. How many times do we need to burn our hand on a hot stove before we become nervous about approaching a stove?

Conversely, I have worked with and treated a number of officers who were hypersensitive and hyper-vigilant about possible physical threats to them. It is these officers who are more likely either to rush into actions that could have been avoided by proper application of patience, or, through some tension-filled behavior, to escalate the severity of a confrontation that could have been avoided by employing a quieting and relaxed demeanor as a part of their tactical response.

Training for Maximal Performance

What we do every day becomes familiar to our brain; what is familiar we perceive as normal. For police officers, normalcy feels good because it allows them to relax somewhat the subtle, usually subconscious, continuing tension associated with maintaining vigilance. Many develop a tendency to reduce stress by anticipating or predicting all the parts of the incident they will encounter.

Police officers base such predictions on all the past times when they have encountered a certain type of event, or particular conditions, and have found some specific manner for handling them successfully. As they go along in their career, they develop a style of policing, or, put in technical terms, a response-patterned behavior, that is habitual and highly likely to occur as an automatic reaction to a relatively wide range of tactical conditions.

This is not effective tactical planning, because the officer is concentrating his or her attention upon past events instead of being vigilant and completely focused upon the current encounter. Such a response tendency serves police officers badly, because pre-judging a contact instead of analyzing the contact means they will be mentally unprepared for unusual, unanticipated, rapidly changing, or chaotic conditions.

By the time officers have encountered scores of burglaries, for example, they have developed a response that has proved successful and that they are comfortable with. When they hear the radio call or penal code number dispatched for a burglary, they are often already telling themselves: "Oh, it's going to be one of *those*. This is what I'm going to find when I get there."

When the circumstances an officer is about to encounter are unknown or uncontrolled, the officer is likely to have an uncomfortable feeling, akin to a premonition that something bad will happen. This tension creates an imbalance in the body's equilibrium, and the mind uses automatic psychological defenses to reduce that tension. The mental scenario an officer may play, in which the unknown elements appear and the officer visualizes himself or herself reacting in a positive manner, is one such defense mechanism. These visualized scenarios make officers feel better, because they are able to predict what they will encounter and feel better prepared.

However, when an officer expects a certain set of conditions and the encounter turns out to be different, rapidly changing, or chaotic, the officer may suffer a perceptual lag that results in a short-term cessation of conscious thought, usually in the form of a startle reaction that can cost valuable time and lives. Predictions about what they will find may be comforting to officers, but they lessen the likelihood that those officers will put in the time and energy to consistently train and condition their minds to make tactical analyses and decisions, and to develop a range of possible responses through the body of knowledge they have learned. When police officers prejudge the incident they are about to encounter, they are, whether they are aware of it or not, wagering that this current incident will permit them to use methods that have worked in the past without severe consequence. The stakes are too high for such a wager.

In order to develop the adaptive expertise needed in such circumstances, officers must possess a deep comprehension of the conceptual nature of the problems they will encounter (e.g., understanding the dynamics and differing characteristics of the various types of assaultive behavior). Training efforts must provide a conceptual model that assists the officer in understanding both how things work and why they work. Accurate models improve performance of complex tasks, and, conversely, inaccurate models decrease task performance (Cannon-Bowers and Salas, 1998).

These training efforts must occur under conditions of moderate adversity, because stress exposure training habituates or "teaches" the "thinking" brain to remain focused and purposeful under conditions of stress. In the absence of such training, the introduction of stressful conditions to the brain results in an immediate "shift" in brain activity. Neural activity in the part of the brain that analyzes situations, prioritizes the circumstances to be dealt with, and makes decisions—the "thinking brain"—is lessened substantially. The "spark and fuel" for brain activity is shifted into the "reactive brain" in order to perform survival or adaptive responses.

Training must first address normative, ongoing situations that will be frequently encountered in interactions with resistive or dangerous subjects. Thereafter, variability, ambiguity, and inconsistencies have to be inserted into the task to force trainees to stretch their learning to a level of competence that permits them to rapidly respond to difficult or unanticipated events. The adaptive process only occurs when the material that is presented is just beyond the trainee's level of experience and current knowledge. Solving the problems presented in the training then requires trainees to stretch their ability and adapt their knowledge to new information and skills (Cannon-Bowers and Salas, 1998).

Police officers must have ongoing practice in dealing with the highly complex and often conflicting stressors encountered at a crime or civil (e.g., domestic) scene so that appropriate skills are both developed and maintained over time. Such skills are perishable. Without this crucial practice, one cannot expect the officer to attain maximal performance of the tasks necessary to achieve officer safety and proper control of a scene (see also Cannon-Bowers and Salas, 1998). Some aspect of the officer's tactical response will be compromised.

Trainees need long-term, guided, and extensive practice in tactical response, and the opportunity to develop the necessary skills in an organized but flexible structure. Because emergency or crisis events contain highly stressful conditions, exposing trainees to stressful conditions while they are practicing in event-based training will enhance the likelihood that officers will react decisively and accurately during a stressful event. Training efforts that are performed under low-stress conditions will not likely be replicated by officers' actions in the field (Cannon-Bowers and Salas, 1998).

The adult education model currently practiced in most U.S. Police Academies does not structure the educational process sufficiently to replicate the adverse, usually unpredictable, and often confusing ways in which information becomes available to officers in the field. It is based upon a more predictable, stable provision of procedural skills—excellently done in the classroom, but, at times, somewhat less so in the area of preparing new recruits to effectively control real-time problems under conditions of emergency.

Take, for example, the phenomenon of sensory distortion that occurred in close to seven out of every ten lethal force contacts by patrol officers I have debriefed over a period of twenty years. During moments when the officer encountered unanticipated, rapidly changing, or chaotic conditions for which he or she was not mentally prepared, he or she would be highly likely to experience changes in the perception of sound, vision, memory, and conscious awareness. The impression that a suspect was moving in slow motion, the narrowing of one's vision to a minute part of the stimulus field, the seemingly diminished sound of gunfire going off, and errors in judgment of distance and position are some of the perceptual distortions experienced by a large percentage of officers that were involved in shootings. To the extent that they had not been made aware of the effects of stress upon the brain during emergency conditions, or learned and practiced simple methods to prevent such distortions from occurring, officers were more likely to experience a perceptual shock reaction during moments of crisis.

The shock reaction felt by the officer during moments of crisis does not cease at the end of the contact. The symptoms developed in

Post-Traumatic Stress Disorder that have afflicted many in law enforcement began as shock reactions created because the officer was not mentally prepared for what he or she was about to encounter.

Marty was a great street cop, and had been promoted to detective and assigned to the Narcotic Special Investigation Unit. He was on an undercover assignment, posing as a buyer of stolen motorcycle "choppers" from members of an outlaw motorcycle gang. An informant had arranged a meeting between Marty and the bikers that would take place in the parking lot in front of a strip mall. The informant now sat with Marty in a pickup truck in the parking lot. Marty's partner and best friend Phil waited in a car on one of the streets adjoining the parking lot, and another member of their unit, Bob, was parked on the other adjoining street. Both were accompanied by several other backup investigators and officers.

It had been arranged with the bikers that only one of them would approach the pickup truck. The bikers had been told that this was because Marty was nervous about having all the money for the stolen choppers with him.

At a corner of one of the businesses, two bikers were arming themselves with a number of weapons they had hidden in the trunk of their car. With the weapons hidden on their bodies, they both turned and approached Marty's pickup truck. "Uh oh," exclaimed Marty to the informant, "tell them just one of them . . . just one of them." There is always a "bust signal" in a case like this one, some event or action to signify that all the officers should rush in to make the arrest. The "bust signal" in this case would be given when the biker got to the pickup. All the backup officers were to rush in then to apprehend the lot.

When Marty saw that both suspects were approaching him, he spoke into the wired microphone he wore, notified all backup units what was happening, and called out to the bikers, "Just one of you is good, just one of you." This part of the plan was of great importance for Marty's safety, because the informant was unarmed, and having to contend with two suspects would place Marty in much greater danger. Marty's shotgun was lying across his lap. The biker's response to Marty's and the informant's requests for only one of them to approach was to say, "Get f—d."

One of the bikers approached the pickup truck ahead of the other and looked into the truck's cab. He saw Marty's shotgun and appeared to become enraged. He began screaming at him: "Go for it, go for it, punk, don't threaten me with a gun!"

Marty tried to calm him: "Here it is," he said, holding out a stack of money, "just take the money." The biker paid no attention to the money or to Marty: "Go for it, motherf—r, go for it!"

At the moment he saw this happening, Phil leaped out of his car, slammed the door shut, and yelled, "Call 'em in!" The day was hot, the windows of Bob's car were closed for the air conditioning, and he did not hear Phil. Bob thought for an instant that Phil was just getting a closer view, so he was delayed for a number of seconds. When he saw that Phil did not stop at the fence bordering the parking lot, but instead turned the corner and attempted to make contact with the suspects, Bob got out too and ran for the lot.

The biker who was screaming at Marty yanked the door open and pulled a revolver from his right rear waistband. The second biker turned and ran around to the front of the truck. Phil ran onto the parking lot and was confronted by the second biker, who was pointing a .44 caliber four-inch revolver at him.

As Phil began to point his weapon at the biker and yell, "Police, freeze. . . . Police, freeze," his vision narrowed drastically, focusing on the cylinder on the suspect's gun. He saw the cylinder begin to turn and the suspect's finger pull the trigger. The biker fired twice, and Phil fired three times. Phil saw the biker jerk as he was hit three times by Phil's fire. The biker ran toward the passenger door of the pickup truck and then went down out of view.

While all this was happening, the first biker was leaning in and pushing at Marty, who was yelling, "He's got a gun. . . . Hey man, there ain't nothing gonna happen," still trying to defuse the situation as the biker began shooting into Marty's upper body and head, still screaming, "Go for it, motherf—r, go for it!"

Phil turned toward the windshield and fired four times. The second biker was now standing at the back of the truck, and they started firing at each other, ducking up and down. As he exchanged gunfire with the second biker, Phil was also firing into the window of the pickup truck, trying to get the first biker to back off and away from Marty. The second biker began to turn and run away from the truck, because Bob had now arrived at the scene and fired two times at the second biker.

Bob now observed the first biker backing out of the truck's cab holding a gun, and fired three times into the biker's back. Bob ignored another shot at him from the second biker as he stood looking at the primary suspect that he had just shot.

Both Phil and Bob now saw the second biker raise his hands and walk towards Bob, saying, "I give up. Don't shoot, I give up. I've been hit." Bob ordered the second biker to a felony prone position, a safety procedure for officers dealing with dangerous persons, and Phil acted as his backup.

It was at this point, after the immediate threat had ebbed, that the ugly reality awaiting them slammed into Bob and Phil. Bob ran up to the driver door of the truck and looked in at Marty, closely followed by Phil. Phil opened the passenger door and held Marty's body. There was a loud snoring sound coming from Marty, and a large entry hole in his forehead.

Within a period of seconds, one police officer had been murdered, another wounded, and over twenty-seven shots fired by four different guns.

Most police officers, as previously noted, tend to predict the details and outcomes of a contact before they ever arrive (Deuel,

2001). Even though police officers always go into their work armed, even though they may have many years of experience in the field, no police officer expects to be holding his best friend in his arms, staring at a hole in his forehead. Even though these three officers were veterans of great ability and reputation, neither Marty nor Phil nor Bob had been mentally ready for what they encountered.

It is probable that Marty's ability to save himself was limited by the role he was playing in his undercover assignment. He had to pretend he was a crook, and so he could not use any of the procedures he'd learned at the Academy and in Field Training.

The greatest injury suffered by Phil and Bob was their helplessness to save their best friend and partner, Marty. Even though they had gone over and over their plans, even the most detailed police plans can change right in the middle of operations.

Phil could not recall a number of things that had happened during the incident: "There is no way I ever thought that I fired fourteen rounds . . . no way in hell. I had to have fired fourteen rounds because I checked them before I put them in there. . . . You are talking about the difference of a second here and a second there and shooting going on and people moving so quick you can't believe it, and you are trying to remember, you know, he was here a second ago, now he is over there, he was shooting, and now he's not."

It had all seemed unreal to Phil, with everything moving in slow motion. "Everything was functioning, but it seems like I wasn't telling it to function. When a guy is standing there and he has a gun on you . . . I can remember looking right at his hand; it narrowed that much that I could just see the gun in his hand. I was firing at suspect two and as soon as he went down I could hear Bob screaming at Marty. He must have been yelling all the time, but I never heard it until suspect two went down."

Phil continued to be haunted by his helplessness to save Marty. He was often overwhelmed by feelings of guilt, thinking that he should have done more in the incident than he had been able to do.

The emotions and thoughts that haunted Phil throughout the rest of his career and into his retirement began as freeze frame reactions, created by sensory shock he experienced when he saw the situation deteriorating and felt an extreme dread for his buddy Marty. Bob left police work shortly thereafter, and carries the memories of Marty's murder with him to this day. Memories of Marty accompany them as much as they now accompany Marty's two daughters whenever they do any of the special things that a daughter does with a Dad.

Fighting Instinct with Preparation

Unfortunately, the skills learned in Academy training, the expectations developed by Field Training Officers, and the desire of the individual officer cannot always be expected to overcome the brain's instinctive response to an extreme threat. During circumstances in which an individual is forced into a position of disadvantage, he or she may experience feelings of helplessness, isolation, or defeat. For officers to survive and to perform according to the rules promulgated for them, they must overcome a human survival instinct that has existed as long as there have been predator and prey—the phenomenon of **conservation withdrawal**.

Many people are familiar with the concept of the "fight or flight" response. However, like the proverbial "deer in headlights," most human beings (except for those employed in law enforcement or the military) are just not mentally or physically prepared to engage in violent combat as their response to an encountered threat. The much more likely human responses will likely be either an attempt to escape the threat ("flight") or passivity. The initial, primitive mechanism used as for survival by prey animals under grave threat involved conservation withdrawal, an instinctive quietude. By becoming and remaining still and quiet, the animal does not attract predatory assaults against itself.

Not all officers possess a confident, dominant, competitive, "refuse to lose" personality they can call upon to ensure victory during a felonious assault against them. Indeed, I have witnessed, during an observation of "simunitions" training (filled with paint, the munitions sting without causing serious injury), officers falling down and stopping any aggressive action when a paint ball struck them—even when the paint ball had struck them in the arm, shoulder, or leg. Officers need to be taught that pain is no barometer of how badly you are hurt. If an officer is unprepared mentally and physically for a life-or-death struggle, then the pain and shock of being struck by a bullet could well result in a lessening in the intensity of fighting for his or her life as a conservation instinct.

To countermand this instinct, police officers must be conditioned or habituated to adverse conditions from the earliest moments of their training. There is just no other means to ensure that the "lowest common denominator" in the skill level of police officers will be adequate to properly resolve any conditions that they encounter.

A number of officers who have survived gunshot wounds they suffered during assaults have described their belief about what it takes to maintain the will to survive. They unanimously describe the importance of the continuous mental preparation they underwent prior to the encounter. They say they had conditioned themselves for what might happen to them and what they would do if struck. They had determined that they would deal with the pain later but concentrate on surviving at that moment: "Deal with the pain later. . . . Now's the time to survive" (Lim, 2001). Furthermore, they expected to win. They did not permit personal difficulties, relationship problems, fears of departmental or media scrutiny, or fear of punishment for using lethal force to limit or govern their aggressive response to a threat. Officers I have interviewed who successfully defended themselves against lethal assaults have reported that they were competitive individuals, and did not accept losing at anything. They were mentally and physically ready when the threat was encountered. The others are dead.

In response to an egregious wound against the body, the parasympathetic nervous system shuts down the body's ability to continue extreme physical exertion, to protect itself from engaging in some act that would result in excessive injury. When officers fail to engage in purposeful, willful, and intentional mental and physical activity during a fight for their life, such as when they experience a "this is too much for me" psychological response to being wounded, their body can shut down, and they will die.

Willful activity in the brain prevents the occurrence of shock reaction, because shock and a feeling of helplessness are antithetical to purpose and intent. This purposeful activity of the brain prevents the parasympathetic nervous system from shutting itself down by activating the sympathetic nervous system, the one responsible for energizing and arousing one to action.

In a true story taken from *Force under Pressure: How Cops Live and Why They Die* (Blum, 2000), an officer was faced with just such a severe assault. It may be that the words of one Academy instructor made the difference between fighting for his life and giving up.

The crook was called the "John Wayne Bandit." He had hit many of the major restaurants in the city. He had been given his name because each time he struck he became bolder and more aggressive. It had reached the point where he'd kick the doors, shoot his gun into the ceiling to scare patrons, pistol-whip the manager, and generally terrorize people. However, by the time officers responded to the call, he would be gone. This had been going on for two and a half years.

An analysis of where the crook had struck suggested that there would be another hit soon, although patrols were told not to engage the crook directly at the scene but go to where they thought he would go after the event. Restaurant managers were provided with alarms controlled by a remote button held by the manager. Pushing the remote button superseded all normal radio transmissions to report, "Armed robbery in progress" and give the name and location of the restaurant.

Herb was doing an overtime shift, trading duty watches as a favor to a friend. He was twenty-seven years old and had ten months on the job. His excellent police work had given him a good reputation in a very short period of time. Others in patrol gave him the nickname "shit magnet," because things happened whenever he made a stop. If he asked for backup, other officers knew there was a felony involved. "After a while," he told me, "everyone in the city would roll when I requested backup because they knew something 'good' was going to happen."

Herb had a report pending from the day before, when he had arrested two burglars leaving a condominium complex. It was a drizzly, cold night and he was cruising a residential area. "I wasn't intending to do anything that would give me any extra work," he told me. "I had this report holding and it was overtime. I had just requested permission to come into the station, finish the report and end the shift. I received permission to come in and finish up. All of a sudden the emergency channel reports a "211" (armed robbery) in progress at _____ restaurant. I went, 'Oops, it's right across the street.' "

"I responded to a residential tract behind the restaurant," he continued, "remembering what the detectives had told us. I was anxious. . . . I wanted to catch this guy. Having the rep of 'shit magnet' was a burden. If you get involved in something good it's an adrenaline rush itself. Plus [there's] the satisfaction of other officers saying, 'way to go.' "

Herb hit his "kill" switch, extinguishing all lighting in or on his patrol vehicle. He began to cruise slowly. As he turned southbound, he saw someone walking to a car. "That's him," Herb said. "Not a 'possible.' That's him. In my mind there was no question." The suspect entered a vehicle and headed south at about twenty-five miles per hour. His vehicle was driving without any lights.

97

"We're both going southbound. I don't think he's seen me yet. But we go under a streetlight and I think it illuminated me. The suspect's lights go on and he speeds up. He doesn't stop for the stop sign. I put out 'possible suspect fleeing' and give my location. I'm thinking, 'The race is on. This is where it gets to be fun. We're going to have a good pursuit. And nobody gets away from me.'

"You have to appreciate the fact that at ten months, you're doing so well you get that sense of invulnerability. And you get that big 'S' [Superman sign] on your chest like 'Everyone is going to submit to me or lose to me.' That is the kind of feeling I had.

"I got on the gas . . . put my lights on. The suspect turned right at the corner and I made a right-hand turn to follow him. I was surprised by the suspect. . . . The suspect had stopped. . . . He was waiting for me.

"Then he took off again, slowly. I went, 'Whoa, what is it with this guy? He's not playing by the rules. He's supposed to run, and I'm supposed to chase him and get the cavalry on him and then we all chase him.' I know that something is wrong . . . that this is not normal. . . . We're going really slow."

Herb began to assess the local streets and possible avenues of escape the suspect might choose. He still had the mindset that the suspect was "waiting to make his move to get away."

The officer put out his information and location again, and cited the suspect's license plate. He hoped that his transmissions would bring the 'cavalry': "I'm confused because I look at my rearview mirror and there's nobody there. I wasn't getting any response back. This confused me. When you're the shit magnet and everyone's coming at every one of your stops and all of a sudden nobody's there . . . why? I thought I was doing everything right."

The suspect again changed his behavior. "All of a sudden he's on the gas. He makes a right turn and, it's like, OK, now the chase is on.

"Well, I make my right turn at a high rate of speed and as I come around the corner he had stopped. He sucked me in big time. Man, that's not the way the game is played. I get this big, 'oh shit' feeling. I know at that point it's going to be a shooting. I even visualize myself in the shooting before it happens.

"I knew that I was going to be shot. 'I better prepare, I've got to do something.' It was a fear. After feeling the fear then I stepped into another stage: 'I'd better prepare myself.' " Herb reached down, unsnapped his holster, and said, "OK. Here's what I want to do. I want to get my gun, have my door open, and move into a position of defense behind the door and at the frame of the car in the 'V.' "

Because of the imminent combat, Herb began to experience some distortion in his senses: "Everything was so slow . . . I thought I had lots of time for thinking this. In a very short time that's what I did. I told myself all the things I wanted to do."

At that moment, Herb suddenly shifted his focus and recognized the need to contact dispatch again. "This is going to be my last transmission before it happens. I tell dispatch my location . . . what I'm doing. . . . I still get no response. He sees me on the radio. His car comes to a complete stop . . . no brake lights. . . . He either put it in park or . . . the emergency brake. . . . His door comes flying open."

While Herb was engaged in analysis, planning, and concentration, he was moving, without being aware he was doing so, to a position of defense: "Other than pre-programming myself, I have no idea how I got to that position. I can remember being at the door with a gun in my hand and returning fire.

"He's coming at me. I see flashes coming out of the muzzle of his gun. They're pretty significant flashes, not just a little pop. They're thundering in my vision like, 'BOOOMMM BOOOOMMMM,' but I hear nothing. As he's running towards me the first two rounds are supposed to have hit me in the upper chest. They came right over the steering wheel and lodged in the seat but I wasn't there. That's how fast I moved. But one of them did catch me in my right arm . . . the upper bicep.

"I'm returning fire. I didn't feel the one that hit me. Another round splintered and hit me in the head. I didn't feel that one either. The suspect comes running at me. I'm feeling ineffective. I'm throwing rounds out and nothing is stopping him." Although the officer was unaware of it at the time, one of his first two bullets had hit the suspect in the area of the chest and torso.

"He's still coming. Again, that's not how it's supposed to work. He's supposed to be falling and he's not doing it. He comes up and sticks his gun in my car window and shoves the gun at my upper torso and caps off a round. He hits me in my left shoulder and I start to move to my right with the impact, across the seat.

"I see him hit me. I can see him move the gun to my lower torso because he wants to put one in my body. What he winds up doing is hitting my elbow . . . shatters it . . . immediately excruciating pain. My hand hits the seat and my gun goes flying under the floorboard. It's another 'oh shit' feeling. This hurts like a sonofabitch. It doesn't make me less aggressive but it makes me aware of the disadvantage I'm at.

"I see him roll and then come up at the rear of my trunk. I can see him standing with one hand on the trunk . . . his gun pointed at my car. It was a great tactical position for him and I was thinking . . . OK, I'm really feeling hurt. I could feel blood coming down my face. I'm lying there and I'm thinking, do I go for my gun and hope that I'm quick enough to get my gun and try to defend myself? Because he's going to come up for another attack if I do that. If I go for my gun he's going to immediately rush up from his defensive position and come in and it's going to be a gun battle in my car.

"And then I think, there's got to be enough blood on me to where he may think I'm dead. Do I play possum? I make the decision. I remember from the Academy saying, here is where they get you. I just weighed my options. To try to get my gun was not the smartest thing to do. I was badly hurt, and I might not even be able to get it. It was a tactical decision.

"I'm waiting for the shot. I know it's going to hurt. I'm telling myself, 'If he shoots me I will survive. I will. He may shoot me again but it won't be fatal.' You have to have a mental will . . . to program yourself to know that things will be OK. I'm calling upon my instincts to want to survive and win no matter what."

This was a totally new experience for Herb. I asked him what he had called upon, what experience base or mental process had helped him maintain such a powerful will to survive. He thought for a moment. "You know where cops have dreams? Where they can't hit the suspect? I had dreams like that before. I would be running around a corner chasing a suspect, and there he would be when I turned the corner . . . waiting for me . . . stabbing me. . . . I'd wake up scared," he recalled. "I would go, 'OK we're going back to sleep. . . . We're pickin' it up. . . . ' I would go to sleep thinking, 'OK, we're going to win.' I wouldn't go to sleep until I told myself, 'Here's the outcome . . . this is where we win.' I would do that every time I had a bad dream. That's all I can recall that made me draw from that." I told Herb that the mental processes he had instinctively performed in the night were a perfect example of pre-programming himself (through a process of mental rehearsal called visualization) for success.

Now, lying across his car seat with one leg hanging out the door, Herb felt the door open. "I knew he was there. I was anticipating the shot. But the next thing I know, my car is moving, and when my car starts moving I know that he's back in his car and he's gone, because that's the only way my car could start rolling." (Herb's vehicle had been front bumper to rear bumper against the suspect vehicle.)

Herb was severely wounded. "I can remember lying there for a couple of seconds thinking, 'You know, I don't have time to die. I've got too many things . . . I've got kids to raise.' I saw my kids and saw I had to survive. I had to do something.

"And then I remember Bob Smithson [L.A.P.D., Retired, a nationally renowned expert on Officer Survival Training], my officer

101

survival instructor in the Academy . . . . and this man has some tremendous command presence. I remember him standing in front of us, face-to-face close, saying, 'The only cop who dies is the one who wants to die. If you want to live you will live.' And then he told us about certain cops who died with non-vital wounds. It was like he was standing in my car and he said this."

With that recollection of his survival instructor, Herb felt like someone had slapped him. He grabbed the steering wheel with his right hand. He pulled himself up. He sat up in the car and found that he could see the suspect four or five houses away from him, going westward up the street. He looked down, turned on his overhead lights, and went in pursuit of the suspect. The officer put out his call number over the radio, that he'd been shot, and where the suspect was heading.

"What I found out later . . . a major frustration for me was that nothing was getting responded to. It turns out there was bad transmission that night, and the manager kept pressing the alarm that would supersede the normal green channel frequencies, and while he was pressing, my transmissions were being covered. One of the other officers had gone directly to the restaurant and was told to follow a different suspect vehicle in the opposite direction. And he is calling for backup going the other way. He thinks he is following the suspect. Plus, when I fell in my car, I pushed out all the buttons. . . . I wasn't on any frequency."

"I'm very angry. I got angry in the car. Because this guy had done what he did and I felt like . . . if he could do this to me, you know . . . I'm a cop. . . . He's supposed to submit to my authority. He's supposed to let me take him into custody, because I'm a police officer. I'm more than your average citizen . . . and if he does this to me, what's he going to do with the next person? So I got really angry and then even angrier. I punch in my buttons. I see nothing. He's disappeared. Where'd he go? I see him in the middle of a mud field. I put out, 'Here he is.' "

At that point, Herb observed a patrol vehicle from a neighboring city turn the corner. He saw the suspect with his spotlight trying to get out of his car. He started thinking again about what he would do if the suspect came at him again. Herb was in great pain and felt the blood coming down his face. He was confused because he didn't know how it had got there. He could only drive with his right hand, his left being completely incapacitated. He saw the other city's officer exiting his car and approaching the suspect vehicle. (It was later discovered that this officer thought that a person had driven too fast for the wet conditions and had spun out into the mud field. He was approaching the suspect with the intention of assisting him.)

Herb called the other officer back. "I've been shot," he told him. "That's the 211 suspect and I'm on my way to the hospital."

"I turn on my siren and I'm out of there. I have everything going through my mind. . . . If I get to the hospital, everything's going to be OK. . . . I'm talking to myself, telling myself to slow down at the intersection, look both ways. . . . I can't afford to get in an accident. . . . I'm OK."

Herb demonstrated what all who wear the badge strive for during a potentially lethal encounter. He never stopped thinking, planning, and adjusting to an amazing series of frustrating circumstances that left him without communication with any other law enforcement resource. This purposeful action and will activates a part of the brain that engages in the intentional, willful action necessary for the wounded officer to survive.

The suspect bled to death from a chest wound incurred in the officer's first return of fire. In my mind, the officer acted heroically, not because he took the life of a felon in a violent gun battle, but because he did whatever it took to prepare himself for this lethal encounter. Unlike many contemporary police officers, he did not become lazy or complacent with the mental preparation required for officer survival. He never went into shock, because he kept concentrating, thinking, planning, and prioritizing what he had to do. He kept himself moving and acting, and never ceased his efforts against the obstacles to his victory.

Herb is still, many years later, a working police officer, now a sergeant. He loves life and enjoys laughing with his wife (who was also on duty that night as a canine officer) and children. Not surprisingly, he doesn't like it when his radio transmissions get covered.

5. Police Agencies

While most people who hear about the stresses of police work envision incidents encountered in the field (e.g., infant deaths, fatal traffic collisions, innocent victims), which do, indeed, traumatize a sizeable number of officers, the majority of police officers believe that the worst stresses in police work come from within their agencies and organizations themselves.

While it will not be received well in all sectors of law enforcement, the fact remains that a large number of police agencies are, for the most part, dysfunctional systems. The same independent, creative, or forward thinking that would bring material rewards and increased status in a well-functioning business environment could brand a police person as a maverick. In short, to get along, you're supposed to go along.

There is most often some amount of conflict between management and the rank and file of police personnel in law enforcement agencies. On the administrative side, a lament often heard is that the police association does not understand the constraints of funding and the political pressures that are brought to bear upon the agency. The police association often describes the management personnel as "not real cops anymore" and therefore unable to understand what police officers' needs are. When there are divisive elements or characteristics within a police agency, or between the agency and its governing city council, the quality and performance of police work will suffer.

The fact that police agencies operate according to a vertical, military-rank organizational structure ensures that the characteristics of each agency—and the manner in which it is run—will exert a powerful influence upon police performance. What the public must understand is that the success of a police officer or deputy sheriff's entire adult career and livelihood—all his or her efforts to make life meaningful and successful—is predicated upon satisfying and pleasing those in ranks above.

In those police agencies where promotions are based upon merit and are performed according to the strictest standards of fairness, the quest for excellence will drive the performance of all personnel. Where the promotions in an agency occur according to criteria other than performance and ability—such as court-ordered quotas, or the power of individuals in command to reward their allies and punish their opponents—police performance will be influenced in ways that may (and usually do) have unintended and/or undesirable consequences. The desire for personal gain or to avoid negative scrutiny should never be permitted to replace virtue and a drive to excellence as the motivating force in police work.

Unfortunately, few police agencies spend much effort upon motivating their troops and making available the resources that will ensure the most excellent performance by these officers. Indeed, Bernard Parks, the former Chief of Police of the Los Angeles Police Department, upon being queried about the hundreds of police officers leaving the department, stated that it was not "his job" to be responsible for officers' morale. His attitude was, basically, if you don't like the job the way it is, you're an undesirable employee and you should get out. His primary role, he felt, was to enforce conditions mandated in a Federal Consent Decree the city agreed to in order to avoid a Justice Department lawsuit, and to make his officers accountable to their community (*Los Angeles Times*, April 10, 2002).

In other police departments, like the Garden Grove Police Department in southern California, a totally different philosophy of leadership has literally saved the careers of some officers with the immediate commitment of aid and resources. For example, Assistant Chief of Police Scott Jordan has championed an immediate-response Trauma Support Team of police officers to aid fellow officers in the aftermath of tragic events. Chief Joe Polisar began the practice of holding formal ceremonies to compliment and promote employees. It is no accident that the morale and service orientation—as well as the ability to react decisively in tactical encounters—are at such high levels of excellence there.

The standards and criteria by which a police agency holds its employees accountable, and the equity with which all in the agency are supported and held responsible for their actions, will go a long way toward defining the ways in which the police perform their tasks.

Fears of Liability

Among the more serious recent problems impacting police work is the fear of vicarious liability that in large measure controls the policies and performance of contemporary police procedure. In many instances of police contact with potentially assaultive subjects or suspects, fears of vicarious liability by the municipality's government and the leadership of the police department, and the fear of excessive and unfair personal scrutiny, often determines what a police officer or deputy sheriff does in a tactical encounter—more than the tactical elements within the encounter itself, or what is known about effective police action.

One result of recent fears on the part of the police and municipal governments is the power of the mythical belief that lessening aggression in police officers and reorienting their education, training, and policies toward service rather than protection will lower the frequency and severity of police uses of force. Those groups advocating decreases in police uses of force have cheered the alteration in police tactics. However, society generally does not realize that the actual impact of reducing or eliminating aggressive actions and behavior in police officers can backfire.

Handling a person with physical force is a very ugly sight. It just does not look good to have seven or eight officers "gang up" on a drunk and assaultive subject in a bar. Therefore, one or two officers now confront the same subject, with many fewer resources, so they will not appear to be "unfair" or unnecessarily forceful. The problem is that the one or two officers will probably need to use greater amounts of force to control the subject, because a suspect who is intent upon assault cannot be as easily contained by fewer officers. This type of change in police work is not supported by tactical theory and practice.

In recent years police officers have substantially lessened their hand-to-hand physical contact with resistive and assaultive persons in order to present a less aggressive picture to the public. However, control tactics that just don't look nice to witnesses are often necessary in order to prevent greater degrees of harm to the innocent. When officers are reluctant to use such tactics, they often let criminals gain a greater degree of initiative. The danger of this is compounded by the instinctive biological events that govern our physical and emotional reactions to stress. The automatic self-protection reactions that are normal responses to danger in most of us are contraindicated for police officers, who are trained and expected to react to danger in a highly controlled manner. However, when officers feel less confident about the way an incident is unfolding, a defensive biological condition is automatically created within their brain that alters what they do to protect themselves.

If an officer either acts impulsively or delays in responding to an assault against him- or herself or another, either escalating a situation that might have been handled calmly or continuing to use verbal tools with the individual when the tactical situation requires physical force in order to control the threat, he or she loses effective control in the struggle with the assailant. The officer then is likely to feel a sense of urgency to "catch up" to the situation and regain the control lost. This often means he or she will overreact to the conditions, responding impulsively and defensively (in a "fight or flight" reaction) instead of proactively and with control.

While the violent subduing of a suspect by seven to eight officers can resemble something like a hog-tying contest, it is far preferable to having to shoot the individual because he was under the influence of methamphetamine or cocaine and would not be subdued by one or two officers using aggressive verbal skills. One or two cannot manage the kind of controlled encounter that seven or eight can do. However, in the context of today's hyper-vigilant sensitivity towards police uses of force, logic, and physics give way in the face of public attitudes.

Liability and public opinion concerns have resulted in a generalized tendency toward attempts to minimize demonstrations of aggression in law enforcement. Three years after the massacre at Columbine, Colorado, for example, the accusation remains among some parents of the victims that the police inappropriately delayed any aggressive response against the two youthful shooters for three hours, while students and teachers were inside dying (*Los Angeles Times*, April 20, 2002).

In a wealthy city in California, a botched robbery in a jewelry store had resulted in the neighboring sheriff's Special Weapons and Tactics Team being deployed. The municipal chief of police refused to allow the sheriff's snipers to shoot the suspect during a period when the suspect was placing hostages in a position to protect him from the surrounding police. He was not going to permit any actions to occur that might give his highly publicized city a "black eye." The S.W.A.T. team's operatives and commander have told me that they are still haunted by the agony they felt as they then watched the suspect kill an innocent woman whom they knew that they could have saved with aggressive police action. They knew that she could have been anyone's mother, wife, or daughter, and they took her loss personally. Society is rarely made aware of the extreme pain felt by officers who witness harm come to the innocent while they were helpless to save them.

The fears of liability and municipalities' efforts at financial risk management have thus reached into police training and practice, especially in the area of physical fitness and training. For example, the amount of time a police department offers officers for sparring and ground fighting practice is most often minimized due to fears that officers will be injured and create liability for the municipality in the form of workers' compensation claims and lawsuits. However, of all officers' physical altercations with assaultive subjects, close to ninety percent begin in a standing position, but end up being fought on the ground (California Commission on Police Standards and Training, 2001).

Skills in weaponless defense are perishable. If they are not practiced continually, with coaching and mentoring provided to ensure that proper methods are being used, they diminish significantly. Knowing this, officers or deputies who contact an assaultive or resistive person are likely to defend themselves with the use of more force than may be necessary, because they lacked the confidence to gain control through hand-to-hand methods.

It is irresponsible for police departments to rely on the personal experience of new recruits to prepare them for hand-to-hand combat. Since many entering police work today have never been in a physical altercation or been struck in the face in anger, encounters with physical threat are likely to result in officers reacting in an instinctive as opposed to controlled manner. Officers' readiness for a highly dangerous part of their role will be compromised if sufficient preparation is not ensured by police policy, selection, supervision, and training. Even though police uses of force occur in only about one percent of all contacts with the public, that one percent amounts to 500,000 incidents per year in the United States (Federal Bureau of Investigation, 1992).

Out of all the uses of police force, at least four times as many occur in an arrest situation as in a non-detention contact, and with persons who challenge police authority (Human Rights Watch, 1998). It is difficult to discern from the literature which police uses of force were applied to assaultive/resistive and dangerous suspects, versus those whose crime was "contempt of cop," yet this distinction is crucial for policy makers of police actions. In the first case, police officers properly react to a criminal threat they encounter in the course of their work, and the severity of force applied is measured according to the severity of the subject's assaultive action (often called the Continuum of Force for Police Officers). In the other case, someone who was given the authority of law violated an individual's civil rights with some idiosyncratic and improper behavior. There is a great deal of bias in this debate, and the literature, unfortunately, bears this bias out. The difficulty emerges in determining which uses of force should be confronted with discipline and punishment and which should be considered appropriate and reinforced as such by departmental commanders.

Discipline and Punishment
Individuals in a police agency hold vertical rank of authority over those subordinate to them. Those in positions of administrative or investigative authority—be they supervisors, commanders or managers, or executives—can, in addition to performing reasonable investigative and supervisorial/disciplinary actions, affect officers' very ability to concentrate and act by improperly or punitively applied discipline (e.g., indulging a personal vendetta for a slight made years earlier, or letting an officer off without discipline because that officer has supported the supervisor politically).

When a police officer is the subject of a citizen's complaint, he or she will be investigated for, sometimes, twelve to fifteen months until a finding is made by the department's Internal Affairs. During that period of time, the officer's vigilance and concentration in the field is highly likely to be degraded somewhat by a preoccupation and distraction with being investigated and subjected to the distressing experience of "waiting for the axe to drop." All a citizen has to say is that he or she was intimidated by the way a police officer was standing, and that officer—at least in one large, urban southern California police agency—could be deprived of a requested transfer and an earned promotion for over nine months. The officer in this case told me that he had been standing with his arms folded on his chest when he responded to the scene of a civil dispute.

The contemporary response of police organizations to an officer who has violated policy is usually to inflict some financial punishment. For misconduct, the punishment is usually a number of days of suspension, or a demotion in pay steps or rank. However, officers are rarely forced to correct the deficit, inaccuracy, or impropriety that resulted in the violation. Therefore, it is probably a misnomer to refer to the practice as "discipline," since this term implies a corrective response to the problem and a precipitant to change.

The attempts by police officer associations to protect officer rights against excessive or capricious punishment have resulted in a number of states developing a Police Officer Bill of Rights (see for example Assembly Bill 301 in California). One of the rights in the Bill guarantees officers a hearing with legal representation present to minimize the severity, or fight the rationale, of the discipline ordered by the chief executive officer. In practice this means that the police agency conducts an Internal Affairs Investigation over a much greater area of perceived or alleged police misconduct, so that all aspects of the investigation are done "by the book," and the officer or deputy arrives at his or her disciplinary hearing with an attorney or union representative to engage in what is essentially plea-bargaining. How in this formalized process is the lesson of the supposed misconduct to be learned? The benefits of valuable corrective action that clearly could be made available in police agencies are lost.

There are, fortunately, bright rays of hope in a number of police organizations. Some enlightened leaders are disciplining officers who were found to have acted improperly by implementing an Employee Performance Improvement Plan (PIP). The PIP has proven much better than punishment, because it makes explicit the areas requiring improvement or mitigation and clearly specifies the responsibilities of the officer and the agency. In some cases, as cited earlier in this chapter, it has saved a number of officers whose careers would have been unnecessarily curtailed in most other departments, but who have corrected their problems and are now viable, vibrant, high-functioning, and professional officers loyal to their organization and community.

These officers kept their jobs because the specific resources required to correct or improve areas of need were identified and provided at the department's expense. While many more agencies claim that their employees are their most valuable assets, these agencies, and leaders of similar character, make that claim true.

The police agencies that function the best have a clear vision of what law enforcement means in their jurisdiction. They follow a Code of Ethics that leads them toward the best in human services. Executive officers of these departments all communicate a simple method for facilitating excellence in responsible police work. They create and promote an organizational climate in which all members of the organization—at every rank—are equally accountable for all aspects of the performance of their responsibilities and duties. When officers can trust that procedures and disciplinary processes are applied fairly and equally—that everyone in the organization will be held to the same standards—they are motivated to perform at high levels, because they are just as often and as strongly recognized for the excellence of their commitment to their community, and to the detection and apprehension of criminals, as they are disciplined for rule or policy violation. Officers in these agencies develop assertive and effective community service, and foster sound political and financial arrangements with outside government and community systems. They exhibit very high morale, as well as a demonstrated impact upon crime and the quality of life in their communities.

In most cases, a police organization's health is left up to individual police executives to ensure or to ignore, and little in the way of public scrutiny is applied to the impact of the organization upon the individual officer. The functioning level and health of a police agency, and its influence upon police behaviors, needs to be included in any societal effort at improvement in law enforcement. Most police executives can produce flowery rhetoric about how important their employees' well-being is to them, but not as many actually follow up their contentions with actions to ensure such wellness. However, in my interviews with several chief executive officers[1] who lead medium-sized to large police agencies and sheriff's departments, each maintained that the manner in which people were treated within the agency was most important, because such treatment would, in large measure, determine how their officers or deputies would treat the recipients of its services.

---

1. Chiefs of Police Joe Polisar, Garden Grove Police Department; Randy Narramore, Huntington Park Police Department; G. "Steve" Simonian, Los Angeles County District Attorney's Bureau of Investigation.

6. Ethics and Politics in Law Enforcement

The ethics of police work, in particular the need to root out corruption, is a frequently raised issue in debates about the police. Ethics is the science that explains the process of forming human values. Ethical values, when articulated about law enforcement, provide the reasons for judging one action by a police officer good and another bad.

It is important to remain aware that all ethical ideas filter through the individuals who perform the tasks and actions that make up law enforcement and constitute the culture of the police agency. Therefore, it is within the context of the values and actions of those who perform police work and police management, and of the characteristics and organizational culture of the police agencies they work in, that the ethics and values of law enforcement should be understood.

Police departments are beset by complexity, pressure, and conflict from the inside and the outside. On the most basic level, law enforcement must comply with the Constitution of the United States, the Bill of Rights, the laws of the state in which the enforcement occurs, and the policies (rules, prescriptions, and proscriptions) of the agency authorized to do what is necessary to protect and serve society. These laws and rules provide the authority for police to perform law enforcement activities, and the policies within police agencies are used to determine how those who make up the agency are to act. In practice, police work quickly presents dilemmas for those who serve, who must at times choose between the rights of the individual and the pragmatic realities of maintaining order, stopping crime, and administering justice. In addition, personal, political, and cultural needs intrude into how police agencies function, and into the tasks and activities for which these agencies are responsible. While the media often appears to view police agencies as entities unto themselves, the reality of how policing is done in local jurisdictions includes a multitude of influences: for instance, federal funding allocations that provide for special community programs but may not maintain a police force of sufficient size to adequately patrol the city or county. City and county governments often complain that there is not enough money.

A part of the problem between the public and law enforcement, though it is difficult for most to observe due to the insular nature of most police agencies, involves the way in which police departments are trained, supervised, managed, and led. In order to foster and support police agencies that perform ethically, society must come to grips with the powerful influences that act upon the individuals who serve in law enforcement. How these influences are formed and how they are managed will, in large measure, determine how policing is performed within that agency.

Rules and Values

In his essay "Ethics and Police Integrity: Some Definitions and Questions for Study," Stephen Vicchio listed the following moral principles as the core virtues that police must possess: prudence, trust, effacement of self-interest, courage, intellectual honesty, justice, and responsibility (in Vila and Morris, 1999, pp. 285–286). These values all refer to some form of moral absolute. Good actions are not good just because good results typically follow from them. There are eternal moral values and principles that are applicable everywhere; some things are right and others wrong. The moral quality of an act is inherent in the act itself regardless of the consequences that may occur, or the personal needs of the individual performing the action. This can present a powerful dilemma for police officers, who often must decide whether to take a strong position against the prevailing political winds, in support of what they feel is right, regardless of the political flak. It is rare, for example, for a police executive to stand forth and publicly support his or her police officers' actions in the face of public furor over a politically sensitive incident, even when the executive believes that his or her officer did nothing wrong.

Moral values held over time become the norms that characterize the "tried-and-true" laws of one's culture, which can then be codified into rules. In police agencies, ethical ideas in the form of rules range from laws and the court decisions that govern the administration of justice to written policies (e.g., governing the use of authority and force, detention, arrest, and pursuit of fleeing suspects) and disciplinary procedures for rule violations by police officers or sheriff deputies. The logic of rule-based ethics suggests that the same rules apply to all members of an agency, regardless of rank or position.

However, there are practical limits to what laws, rules, and policies can accomplish in ensuring ethical police practices. This is because a rule-based ethical system is better at preventing wrongdoing than at motivating right actions. As Deputy Chief Mike Bildt of the San Bernardino, California Police Department has said, rules prohibit and prescribe specific actions, but they do not provide guidance to individual officers insofar as learning fairness and justice, patience, or compassion. Deputy Chief Scott Jordan of the Garden Grove Police Department has spoken of the importance of law enforcement maintaining a values-based police organization, rather than a rule-based organization that simply responds to problems that have occurred. Only a police system that is driven by and committed to honesty, honor, goodness, and fairness, he believes, can achieve fairness and justice for society. Both he and

Chief Bildt fear that too great a dependence upon rule-based policing will hurt the success of at least some of the moral values listed above.

Rules also cannot really define the total of all the possible, complex behaviors that occur inside and outside of social systems like police organizations. For this reason, groups, organizations, subcultures, and cultures develop a set of norms and repeated habits that dictate how they "should" work and live. These norms are then inculcated in whoever enters the group or agency via the attitudes, values, and behaviors the entering individual observes.

I do not believe that society's judgment of the ethics of the police should be solely based upon whether or not officers follow rules. I believe that virtue in police work—i.e., "doing the right thing"—involves an intrinsic drive or motivation to act in a conscientious, proactive manner, confronting the problems and issues of one's community in a manner deserving of the public's trust, to pursue and perform relentlessly, without compromise, regardless of consequence. Nevertheless, if police officers perform their work according to the rules—and the vast majority of good ones do—then society must again place their trust in, and work alongside, these same officers to enhance community living. However, if police officers take actions that destroy the public's ability to place their trust in them, then they must be removed from those positions of authority.

Ethics and Pragmatism

Even in individuals who begin police work with the best motivations and intent, the perception of a lack of support from the community they serve when sensitive incidents occur will soon result in a greater degree of pragmatism. Over time, or because of one very powerful event, humans adapt to the social and environmental conditions they encounter. A major purpose of the adaptive instinct is protection of the individual's viability in any environment that is threatening to them. To protect ourselves from environmental and social stresses, we rely upon certain psychological defenses.

As soon as an individual working in a police organization allows pragmatism to conquer his or her sense of mission, causing him or her to place personal needs before virtue, he or she will, with or without conscious awareness, begin engaging in some form of defensive behavior. Some will withdraw from and avoid their duties when they can; others will become aggressive and confrontational under conditions in which they feel pressured; some will vacillate and some will become immobilized. One should not expect members of an embattled police agency not to develop some degree of degradation in performance of their tasks.

The pragmatic leader translates his or her personal values into norms for behavior, and then codifies the norms into prescriptions and proscriptions for all within the department to follow. These codified rules become law and policy for the organization. Law and policy define what is good and bad; therefore, the leader's logic may run, "Good means compliance with my values and the way I want things done. Non-compliance with the rules of the organization when I am in control is bad."

What is important in determining ethical police work, especially within its leadership, is not a person's need for personal aggrandizement or his or her views on transient issues, but rather his or her character. One cannot legislate honor, kindness, or virtue in policies or written rules. Individual leaders either possess or lack these traits by virtue of their character. Once true character is revealed, policies and actions become predictable and a repeated, relatively stable feature of the organization.

I have been fortunate to meet a goodly number of police executives who dedicate their lives to public and organizational good, rather than their own self-interest. Unfortunately, there are also many who seek only to "survive one more day" in office and are motivated to a much greater extent by self-protection and "not making waves." This distinction can make a significant difference in how those police agencies function (Narramore, 2002).

The achievement of ethical police practices requires individuals of character who understand very clearly what it means to lead, contribute, and perform with excellence and mission. They are driven to perform according to the virtue they carry within. Their acts are influenced and formed by rules, certainly, but are accomplished by their decision to perform their duties according to what is right, even though the consequences of doing so could be extremely severe. The results of this kind of leadership upon police departments and their communities will hopefully be seen in a higher level of morale in police officers and fewer "flare-ups" of temper between police officer and citizen.

The Impact of Politics upon Police Work
Each social system runs on both formal rules and informal norms. Politics are the informal practices within human organizations in which persons or groups act to enhance or advance a position or office for some benefit. This normal social behavior is an inherent component of the system of government within which police organizations operate, and strongly influences their policy and performance.

The interaction between politics and police ethics can be traced through the police agency's vision, mission, values, and policies. A police agency's vision sets its sight on the department's ultimate direction. The agency's mission statement characterizes the positions it takes. Its values are intended to guide the officers in their everyday behaviors and are codified into policy statements, rules to which officers and deputies are held accountable.

"A police chief looks out of a multi-paned window," said Joe Polisar, Chief of Police of Garden Grove Police Department in southern California. "In one pane are the rank-and-file employees, in another the command staff, the elected body, community members; every one affects [the] decision making; all panes are political, with ramifications for every decision made." If, for example, there is a policy that the rank and file are upset about, they will use their influence with elected officials to attempt to get the chief executive officer to change his or her stance. If a citizen or a member of a community organization perceives a problem within the community or with police services, he or she will go to the city council, who will then approach the chief of police to fix whatever problem the individual has identified.

Any discussion of police work should take into account that a police agency is substantially influenced by the actions of elected city or county officials, and the political actions taken by the city council, county board of supervisors, mayor, or city managers will affect the quality of police work in one form or another. The policies within police agencies in which all are told "what to do" are often as strongly influenced by political priorities, and personal values and attitudes, as by the objective needs of the police organization or community itself, identified through some reasonable means of assessment. Should those in power act from personal need instead of the public good, and should the police agency come into conflict with those personal needs, then even an excellent, honorable, compassionate, and heroic police agency can be torn apart. I have personally witnessed this occurrence on more than one occasion.

Any ethical corruption or compromise on the part of elected officials also cannot help but impair the quality of police work. Take the case of a city councilperson who was arrested for being drunk in public. The gentleman had also been driving. He was infuriated that the police would hold him, an elected official, accountable for his actions.

Once a supporter of the police, he now began a prolonged conflict with the chief and other members of the police department who were on his "hit list." The city manager, the city controller, city risk manager, and all the city's department heads resigned, complaining of impropriety on the part of the elected officials. Lawsuits brought by police officers for this gentleman's actions during the subsequent political and personal conflict cost the people of that city several hundreds of thousands of dollars that could have gone for the public good.

At the time this book goes to press, there has been a state takeover of local elections in a municipality where the city treasurer has been arrested and charged with making threats against the lives of others. His supporters on the city council have been "at war" with the police department. The election concerns a recall vote against all elected officials, alleging impropriety and corruption. An individual in the city government who was a critic of this group of politicians was shot and wounded by an unknown assailant. The police association is suing the council and the council is suing the police. The storefront of a business whose owner was assisting the police department in the political drive to institute the recall was firebombed. More than $500,000 from the city's treasury has been spent on attorney fees in a small, relatively poor municipality, and the trials have not yet begun. A striking number of police officers have privately sought help because of severely distressed emotions and disturbed behaviors that have occurred as a direct result of political conflict. In their work environment, the message is clear: don't risk doing any high-intensity police work, because the city council, in order to gain further advantage, will likely use such actions as an opportunity to do further harm.

In other municipalities across the nation, change in population demographics has at times created a series of political conflicts involving shifts of power from one socio-cultural or ethnic group to another. The police agency within such municipalities has been used in these times as a political football punted back and forth as groups vie for positions of political power over others.

The group that gains the majority vote, no matter how slim, will be the one that decides how much the police will be paid to support themselves and their families. Funds required for new police equipment or tools, negotiated working conditions (such as how shift work is organized), and the provision of training resources can be used as bargaining chips in political negotiations.

The only course the police can take that will not compromise their drive toward virtue is to be apolitical while also being politically astute. The chief who avoids being tied to special interests will express respect for all who enter public service without endorsing a specific individual. The chief cannot hitch his or her wagon to a powerful politician and then expect to be free of that politician's influence upon how the police operate. One cannot use one's office to advance a specific political movement without tying how law enforcement is performed to that movement. "The chief who understands that," Joe Polisar says, "will find resolution to conflict. It may not be everything each side wants, but it's a good compromise." Chief Polisar moved to California after working as a police officer in New York and Albuquerque, New Mexico, as the chief. He told me he was initially astounded at the number of chief executive officers in the state who "actually play politics, openly endorsing candidates for political office" (Polisar, 2002).

In any case, suffice it to say that conflicts among the entities that govern municipalities, along with political pressures and motives, are very likely to create dysfunction and discord within a police organization. Conflicts within the police organization are also very likely to lessen the quality of the police work therein, because its officers will be preoccupied by the conflict in the course of their work. Society would do well to shift and expand the focus of its scrutiny for purposes of enhancing law enforcement performance and society's relationship with the police.

Unfortunately, with all the upset directed at police corruption and the need for integrity in law enforcement, less than two percent of the population is observant of, or active within, how government operates. Until the eye of public scrutiny falls sufficiently and with enough frequency upon other pieces of the system of governance, society will be unsuccessful in the complete achievement of its aim of excellence within law enforcement.

Inside police agencies, the interaction between politics and ethics can be traced through the manner in which the leader's vision for police work is translated and implemented by his or her command staff and supervisors. It is not that unusual for a police agency to be fragmented by a number of competing interests whose vision, mission, and values create the same results as a bus being driven with four steering wheels at the same time, with one wheel at each corner of the vehicle.

One event that exemplified the impact of politics upon police work occurred in the riots in south central Los Angeles that took place in 1992, following the acquittal on criminal charges of the four Los Angeles police officers who placed motorist Rodney King under arrest. An outgoing police chief, Darryl Gates, was in political conflict with Mayor Thomas Bradley at the time.

While this is not the place to go into the unfortunate details, politics intruded upon the deployment of Los Angeles police officers and delayed some of the best-trained and most talented police officers in the world during the first critical hours of several days of violent and massive rioting. The delays in deployment resulted in a complete loss of initiative and control for police officers stationed at the "ignition points" of the riots—permitting substantial damage to people and property that could have been prevented.

I later debriefed a police officer from that department who was on duty the first night of the 1992 riots. He told me of the dismay he still felt at the events that occurred during his duty watch on the first night the riots began.

He was assigned to South Central Los Angeles area in the 77th Street substation. Because of delays in the deployment of the department's riot control plan and resources, he provided a crowd control force of one. The next police officer was half a block away; this was how many officers assigned to this patrol sector were available to cope with the surging, looting crowds of rioters and arsonists.

He was about one hundred yards from a Pep Boys auto parts store. A Korean woman, whose family owned the store, had gone to the entrance of her store to plead with the crowd not to hurt her

124

business. The officer heard her screaming as the crowd carried her back into the store, but could not get to her to save her. The sound of those screams has haunted him over the course of a heroic career. No matter how many selfless acts of heroism this man has performed, this is the incident that is paramount in his mind when he thinks about himself and his life as a police officer.

Another impact of political conflict upon police work can be seen in the fact that recruiting, retention, and promotion of personnel in a large number of police departments are at crisis levels. A recent article in the *New York Times* reported that "many officers from the lowest to the highest rank are questioning their occupation, tempted by higher pay in the private sector . . . and discouraged by seemingly constant public and news media criticism about police brutality and racial profiling. 'I would absolutely not take a job as a police chief,' said John Diaz, an assistant police chief in Seattle, who at forty-four already has a good national reputation and is sought after by recruiters for a chief's post. 'The politics of being police chief have become so insane no one wants the job . . . I work an 11-hour day, but our chief is here before me every day and doesn't leave until I'm gone, and all he gets is attacked in the media all the time . . . ' " (Butterfield, 2001).

The current levels of morale in a number of large police agencies are quite low, resulting in a previously unheard-of exodus from all ranks within the agency. The same article noted that there "were only 19 recruits in the [Los Angeles] police academy class in June, a record low . . . and not long before that there were 100 recruits per class. This month [July, 2001] Los Angeles canceled the police academy because there were not enough recruits . . . "

Further, there have been substantial difficulties in making promotions within departments. "In Seattle," the article reported, "the police department is having trouble finding officers to take the sergeants' examination, and sergeants to take the exam for promotion to lieutenant." Lieutenants do not get compensated with overtime pay, while sergeants do.

A number of the officers and deputies whom I interviewed for this book described their feelings about police work. To them, the job of police officer was a calling. They believed that they were meant to perform police work. It was about mission and not money. These men and women sacrificed their own well-being for that of the public, for people they did not even know. Police work was their passion and their life's commitment. These are also the men and women who would react aggressively in the field, and were often criticized for their "dinosaur" attitudes during debates about how police work was performed. Woe be unto society if we permit that feeling of mission to be extinguished in police personnel because they pragmatically defended themselves from the experience of "stoning the keepers at the gate."

I once asked an undercover officer why he did the work he did. He had lost, over time, his previous sense of himself, his wife, and his relationship with his police department. He was upset for a moment, and tears came to his eyes. He then asked me to think about someone attempting to murder my son. He asked me if I would want someone to come and save my son, even if it meant risking injury or loss of his or her own life. I have never asked that question again.

The Politics of Discrimination

There are, in almost every police agency, police officer associations for African Americans, for women, and for Latinos. Their existence illustrates that there continues to be segregation within police ranks, fueled by prejudice and stereotyping.

For example, a police lieutenant in a large, urban southern California police agency approached me and introduced himself as a representative of the African American Police Officers' Association. I had been hired to perform their department's Pre-Employment Psychological Screening Evaluations, and he said his members were interested in speaking with me about my attitudes, beliefs, and approach to my work. I happily agreed to meet with them, as I was enthusiastic about initiating mentoring programs for youths in minority communities to help them develop the characteristic traits, behaviors, and habits that the Psychological Evaluation looks for in the employment of police officers.

He then told me that his membership wanted to know the "racial make-up" of my office and staff. This request ended our relationship. As I have fought, and refused to submit to, racial prejudice of any kind since I started school in 1949, I told him to tell his membership that it was none of their business, and left.

The public must understand that until society does much better at confronting and combating racism in general, the police and the public will continue to suffer from feelings of hurt and anger that lessen any hope of a real rapprochement.

Society has demanded over the last ten years that police departments be more representative in personnel of the communities they serve. The rationale for efforts to make the police more representative of the population was that women and people familiar with the cultures that they might contact in police work would be less likely first to be perceived as a hostile, occupying army, and then to engage in improper actions. Research has shown, however, that women and people of color act no differently than white males do as police officers. In reality, it is not gender or race that are the most important determinants of the police response, but rather situational factors and organizational characteristics (Sherman, 1980). Sherman's findings, as well as the work of others who have studied police behaviors, is of major importance in how law enforcement policy decisions are made. Very little in the way of reform efforts has been applied to increasing officers' adaptation expertise to the range of unusual and/or dangerous situations that they encounter. Instead, reform efforts have focused upon limitations in the police response.

The criteria by which departments hire and promote new police officers and sheriff deputies have been altered during the past ten years in an attempt to respond to internal and external pressures to ensure the proportional representation of gender and race in police officers. Hiring goals have been set to balance the groups that court decisions have determined to have been mistreated in the past. Whether you agree with them or not, these efforts at affirmative action have succeeded in creating a police system that is much more representative of the society it serves than it was previously. For this, I believe that the leadership of law enforcement should be praised for acting on its verbal commitments.

That the field of law enforcement has been in need of change in policies, practices, training, and supervision is not at issue here. Nor will I disagree with the fact that previously occurring injustices in hiring and promotion in law enforcement have to be confronted and corrected. No one should be denied equal opportunity for employment or promotion because of race or sex. Nor should there be alienation, mistrust, and a lack of collaboration between the police and the community. There are, however, problems with training and supervision today that must be adequately addressed if police work is to fulfill its excellent potential for service to society.

While it may be embarrassing to some, the fact remains that the source of a large number of police actions found to be improper—i.e., in violation of department policy—can often be found in deficits in or limits placed upon police training, poor supervision practices by individuals who are unprepared for the tasks of supervision, or officers and deputies who misinterpret or misunderstand laws, rules, and policies.

A deputy brought a lawsuit against her department, complaining that she was improperly being denied the ability to serve on the elite Special Enforcement Bureau of the L.A. County Sheriff's Department. She alleged that she had been told there were no assignments in that unit appropriate for her, and further alleged that persons in authority had told her that she would never be promoted to such a position because she was a woman. She sued the sheriff's department and alleged violation of her Equal Opportunity Rights. The court found for her position and ordered the sheriff's department to "fix" the problem by requiring that a specific percentage of positions of every supervisory rank and authority be filled by a woman before a male could be so assigned.

If the first twenty-five percent of female deputies assigned to Field Training Deputy positions are sufficiently experienced and have demonstrated sufficient competence in the field, then by all means they should be so assigned. However, court-ordered and Consent Decreed assignments raise concerns that, if an individual is not yet ready for one of these critically important training and supervision roles, the assignment will both sabotage the individual so assigned and create the likelihood of some deficit or lapse in the excellent performance of police work in the field. Field Training Officers and Deputies are among the most important influences upon the career-long performance habits and skill levels of all who serve in law enforcement duties. Because there is little career incentive other than increase in pay to remain a Field Training Officer, most use this position as a step on the ladder to promotion. The officers and deputies in the agency with the greatest demonstrated skill in communication (transferring of knowledge and information to another person) should be the ones assigned to train incoming officers and deputies, because it is in this position of training that recruits will learn (or not) the exquisite balance required among the various types of roles and actions that must be taken during the course of police duties.

Some conditions of reward must also be considered to maintain the proper fit of police officer skills to the necessary positions of trainer, teacher, and supervisor. In this manner, more quality people will be motivated to remain in these roles, instead of using them as a springboard to another assignment. If such a system of reward is not forthcoming, the chances are greater that less capable or less motivated individuals will remain in the positions that are the most important in influencing a recruit's subsequent performance as a police officer.

Politics and Police Uses of Force

While the sensationalized incidents that were exposed in the national media toward the end of the twentieth century are most often perceived as the catalysts for change in policing, an incident in Memphis, Tennessee on October 3, 1974 began one of the most significant alterations in police use of force policies. Samuel Walker, an American Civil Liberties Union official and author about police abuses, wrote that "On October 3, 1974, Edward Garner was shot and killed by two Memphis police officers. A fifteen-year-old African American, Garner was 5 feet, 5 inches tall, weighed 110 pounds, and was shot in the back of the head while fleeing police officers." He was later discovered to have taken a purse from a female. His parents sued, and in 1985 the Supreme Court held that the fleeing felon rule, under which the Memphis police justified the shooting, was unconstitutional (Walker, Spohn, and DeLone, 2000, p. 95).

The result of the Supreme Court's decision was a sharp narrowing of the discretion previously possessed by police officers in regard to the circumstances that justified their use of lethal force upon another person. The "defense of life" rule lowered the incidence of police shootings in New York City by almost thirty percent over three years (Geller and Scott, 1992).

The use of lethal force is the ultimate enactment of authority by a police officer. To warrant use of lethal force, an incident has to fit within specific policy guidelines promulgated by each police department—guidelines that are scrupulously engineered to meet the specific legal and constitutional requirements of the department's jurisdiction. The use of lethal force is automatically investigated by the homicide team of the officer's own agency, a shooting review board, and/or the investigators for the county's prosecuting attorney or sheriff.

The use of lethal force must be justified to the officer's supervisors and departmental commanders, the media, community and special interest groups, the officer's peers, and the officer him- or herself. While the legal test for justification of lethal force by police officers varies by jurisdiction, the basic element is this: to be called justified, the use of lethal force by police officers requires that any reasonable person with the training and experience of the involved officer would have perceived lethal threat in the actions taken by the suspect, and thus reasonably have feared for his or her life.

A large number of today's police officers, especially those hired within the past five to ten years, are often hesitant to use even less-than-lethal force on dangerous criminals, sometimes because they fear being second-guessed by a department seeking to avoid vicarious liability for the officer's actions, and by a society that has been ready to convict them for the way they do their jobs.

Many people appear to be under the impression that police officers are well trained to handle each and every circumstance they encounter in the performance of their duties. Indeed, when I have had occasion to provide expert witness testimony in civil and criminal trials in which police officers' actions were being questioned, the attorney opposing the police agency and/or officer would invariably present the argument that police officers should be expected to perform their job without loss of any control—to be free of any impairment in the accurate assessment of the scene and circumstance and the correct choice of action. "After all," the attorney would say, "should we not expect officers to react properly to any and all conditions since they are so well trained in tactical actions?"

The truth, unfortunately, is that while the tactical training provided police officers is generally quite good in this country, the ability of police officers to *use* the tactics that they have learned under conditions of emergency has too often lagged behind the knowledge provided them. The success or failure of tactical training will be determined not by how much the officer knows about police procedure, but rather by how that officer is capable of applying the tactics he or she has learned to the specific conditions encountered.

131

In order to apply their knowledge of tactics to specific field encounters, officers must ensure that they are able to concentrate and focus their attention immediately upon the most important elements at the scene, dismissing elements that are irrelevant to what they must do to take control of the situation.

They must use the information they obtain at the scene in combination with all previous learning and experience they have been provided, and they must perform their response at the rate appropriate to the conditions that they encounter. They must be practiced and mentally ready to apply the appropriate tactics. But where officers are preoccupied or distracted by conditions that are external to the encounter they have at the scene, their analyses of the conditions there can be intruded upon by, for example, their consciousness of a family problem, money owed, and/or the fears of liability that now are infused in a good deal of police training and procedure in this country.

Sometimes it is simply an officer's personality or habitual assumptions that prevent him or her from applying his or her tactical knowledge in a dangerous encounter. It has been documented by empirical research (California Commission on Police Officer Standards and Training, 2001) that a number of officers who were assaulted on duty continued to give only verbal commands to a suspect who was in the act of attempting to murder them. In other studies (Federal Bureau of Investigation, 1994), the characteristics of almost each one of fifty-four murdered police officers were as follows: they looked for the good in people instead of judging them as potentially bad or dangerous; other officers who were asked about the murdered officer noted that they tended to use less physical force, and later in a high-risk incident, than would other officers; and they broke "cardinal rules" of officer safety because they believed that they could read people better than the average officer.

Many police agencies have begun to audit and tabulate all uses of force to evaluate the state of their officer-community relationships, and to hold police officers accountable for their actions. Unfortunately, currently collected statistical compilations do not usually investigate what caused or triggered the officer's use of force, or whether or not such force was a justified response to a subject or suspect's actions.

The danger of using such a global view of police force to evaluate police officers' actions without also analyzing the contributory influences to such action is, in my opinion, that active officers are likely to get a reputation as "magnets" for trouble. They will appear—at least according to the numbers—to be problem officers. In many cases, nothing could be further from the truth. Meanwhile, police work is left undone by officers who do not make enough effort and spend their watch responding to radio calls. Officers who do little don't make waves. No one wants to "tell the emperor bad news."

A surprising number of police supervisors have told me that they are given the message by their commanders to "keep the negative numbers down." Officers are then placed under similar pressure not to put their hands on people, because they will create a stream of report-writing responsibilities on the part of their sergeant and lieutenant, and trigger internal affairs investigations that raise suspicions about the officer. There are a number of departments in the United States today where officers or deputies are more likely to reach for their tape recorder than for their service weapon in a dangerous situation. This behavior is an ineffectual response to the sins of the past, and only serves to put the officer at risk.

Some in special interest groups will not mind if police officers use only verbal command tools regardless of the levels of threat, or if they are hesitant and indecisive in a dangerous encounter, because they are concerned about protection against some form of liability to the municipality, or are active political voices within a disadvantaged community. However, I do "mind." I have sat with widows, fathers, mothers, children, and widowers of officers who had just been murdered in the line of duty, and I will carry their innocent grief and shock with me to the end of my own life.

I believe it is fundamentally unethical for policies to be written demanding that police officers act in a manner that undermines their own safety and gives additional advantage to criminals when there are better ways to preserve the rights of citizens from inappropriate police actions as well as to keep the intervening police officer safe. It is important for society to call for the control and management of *inappropriate* aggression from the police, rather than trying to create a police force that may, indeed, be less able to perform the tasks they were trained in under conditions of emergency. As I have said in an earlier chapter, what we need are not more passive police officers, but better decision makers under stress.

Even with controversy over police uses of force, responsible individuals who represent community action and social service agencies and groups have told me that they are less concerned with uses of force by police officers in the performance of their duty than with the honesty and accuracy of police officers' statements. The concern they reported revealed a lack of credibility they ascribed to police officers because of the misdeeds of a few who had acted improperly, using the color of authority as a cloak for their actions.

There have been incidents of corruption in police agencies that were severe enough to warrant the takeover of the department by the county sheriff. Members of an inner-city police department, for example, were moonlighting as bodyguards for Tupac Shakur and Marion "Suge" Knight, notorious for their gang and crime affiliations in addition to their musical efforts.

Although it is not widely publicized, the infamous Rampart scandal in Los Angeles was indirectly connected to activities involving these gangsters. When criminal police officer Rafael Perez was stealing the cocaine that resulted in his apprehension, the name he used to sign out the drugs was that of a white detective who had shot and killed an off-duty, African American police officer. Neither of the officers involved in the shooting knew that the other was a fellow officer. The African American officer was driving an SUV registered to the wife of Marion "Suge" Knight, who was, at that time, in prison. The white officer was an on-duty undercover narcotics detective whose appearance did not suggest that he was a police officer.

As the story was revealed in the ensuing investigation, the African American officer apparently was angry about how the white officer was driving. A "road rage" encounter ensued. The black officer made a number of threatening statements and gestures and began to follow/chase the white officer, who was transmitting this incident via his radio to other detectives while it unfolded.

At one point, the black officer allegedly brandished a gun at the white officer, who fired his own service weapon, striking and killing the other. There was outrage from some members of the police department, who believed that the shooting was racially motivated. The racism that is endemic to American society was also at work in the Los Angeles Police Department. A prolonged investigation finally cleared the white detective. It is believed that Rafael Perez was caught attempting to frame the white detective for drug theft to avenge the killing of his "homey."

The world was outraged when it became known that a Haitian immigrant, Abner Louima, had been sodomized and beaten by a New York City police officer. In these and other incidents, America was getting a picture of a police force that was lawless in some cases and sexually perverted in others.

There are over eight thousand men and women employed as Los Angeles Police Officers, and over forty thousand who serve the City of New York. The recently publicized misconduct involved less than one percent of all officers on these departments. Yet Americans were made fearful of *any* contact with the police due to the broad-brushed picture of corruption painted by the media.

Thereafter, whenever incidents of possible misconduct were reported, the impression left with the observing public was of unethical, immoral, unlawful individuals who were in positions of power—a truly frightening image. Incidents of misconduct have certainly occurred in law enforcement, but the conditions that actually permitted such misconduct to exist have not been the focus of public scrutiny. Where were the supervisors and commanders, and what were they doing, when Rafael Perez and his partners were taking the law into their own hands?

The department response to the Rampart scandal in the LAPD was to disband the gang unit at the Rampart station. Rampart police officers, especially those in patrol, thus lost a critical source of intelligence and support in their efforts to confront a myriad of community problems with gang crime. It would have been better to ensure effective supervision and command actions in the gang unit to produce high-functioning, high-achievement police actions—casting out the old problems and replacing them with excellence.

To adequately address the issue of police misconduct, one should, I believe, distinguish between incidents that are purposefully or intentionally committed by people of poor character or ethics, and individuals who are poorly trained and supervised and are therefore unprepared for the encounter that is later judged to violate someone's rights. When the public is aware of the difference between these two types of incidents, citizens can exert the pressure of social opinion and attitude upon those individuals and parts of the police organization that truly influence how police work is performed, so that the officers who are intentionally unethical are removed from law enforcement, while the others are properly reeducated via training, mentoring, and supervision.

Impact upon the Officer
Few of the media reports I have read or heard about get to the heart of the crucial decisions and feelings officers experience in a

potentially lethal situation. Not only must the officer worry about an immediate threat, but there are always questions about the consequences of using lethal force.

What will happen to you if you shoot? Will the department support you? Will the jurisdiction you work for simply settle with the suspect's family merely to save on legal fees? Will the department "hang you out to dry" to defend itself from negative media and/or community groups? Will the department be sensitive to what you just went through and show you support, or will you be treated like a suspect?

Will your spouse or loved one comprehend what you went through and what you need after this incident? If you don't shoot, you could be killed. Will the city support your spouse and children? What will be the impact upon your life of responding to a lethal threat directed against you or another innocent person? More and more officers like Chuck, whose story appears below, have begun to question the viability of using the force required by their training in response to a suspect's threatening actions.

Chuck was patrolling a high-crime area in his city at 1:40 a.m. on a cold, clear night. He was working with a partner—an unusual comfort, as his department's patrol division normally worked in one-officer patrol vehicles. He was a skilled police officer and had won the respect of officers many years his senior. While he performed at his best in whatever assignment he was given, his greatest moments were spent going after bad guys and putting them in jail.

Chuck observed a male dressed in black (a color often worn by burglars) looking into a parked truck. At this time of night, and given the actions of this man, Chuck's impression was that the man was an auto burglar. The man saw the police vehicle and began to run directly toward it, a move that surprised both officers. The officers left their vehicle, and the man turned and ran to the rear of the nearest residence. Chuck took on the role of a "chase" officer, quickly told his partner what strategy of communication they should use, and gave chase to the now fleeing suspect.

He saw the suspect leap over a cinderblock wall separating the residences, and called his partner to notify him. He followed the suspect over the wall and chased him through three backyards and over two fences, but then lost sight of him.

Chuck ran to the front of the residence and saw the suspect doubling back. He followed the suspect over another wall, and then called in his and the suspect's probable position to his partner. As he did so, he observed a male, dressed in black, crouched by a tire of a vehicle.

Chuck told the male in both English and Spanish a number of times to show him his hands. The man did not reply to the officer's commands. He then turned towards the officer with a gun in his hand. The incident that had begun with the officer and his partner attempting to apprehend a fleeing criminal had now changed into a face-to-face, life-threatening assault against the police officer.

Chuck shot first. His bullets struck the suspect, who fell upon the gun. Chuck broadcast the shooting and took a position of cover. He saw the gun underneath the suspect's body. He ordered the suspect to show his hands, but the man did not move. Chuck saw the blood spreading out from the suspect's body. Then Chuck's entire world changed.

He approached the suspect and pulled the weapon from underneath the suspect's body. He noticed that the weapon's weight was much less than he had expected it to be. Then he saw the orange tip to the gun's barrel that designated it a replica. Toxicological studies determined that the suspect had been extremely drunk.

A number of years earlier, when Chuck had been a cadet in the same department, he had witnessed a shooting while he was accompanying an officer on a "ride-along." The suspect in that incident had attacked them with a shotgun, so Chuck, seeing the identical features of this weapon, had experience that provided a frame of reference for what lethal threat looked like.

Chuck now felt a renewed concern. He knew in his heart that he had responded properly and appropriately to what any reasonable individual with training and education would have perceived as lethal threat (as noted earlier, the essential legal test for use of lethal force by a police officer). He sensed, however, the beginning fear that the press would have a "field day" at his expense.

At first, Chuck felt that the department's response to him and his family was supportive. His department possessed a Trauma Support Team that was comprised of police officers who had experienced some form of lethal contact and had devoted themselves and their time to taking care of their buddies who experienced similar traumatic events. I had trained them to perform psychological debriefing methods with officers involved in lethal contact, such as a failed attempt at resuscitation, witnessing a suicide, a family killed in a traffic accident, etc.

Chuck felt greatly reassured by the actions of the two Trauma Support Team members who responded to him immediately. "It was comforting to have someone identifying what feelings and reactions I might expect. . . . I knew I had people on my side." He saw the department's response change, however, in response to newspaper banner headlines that read, "Innocent Life Tragically Cut Short."

Representatives of the department had made comments in the story that disturbed him. He feared he was being "hung out" because the department's leadership wanted to comfort the community in which the shooting had occurred. He also became fearful when the department called in the city's human relations committee to study the incident, worrying that individuals with no knowledge of police work or lethal situations would not judge him in a fair and objective manner.

His mother telephoned him, greatly disturbed by the reports she had read that had been so different from his statements.

Demonstrations began in the neighborhood where the incident had occurred. "No way," the demonstrators proclaimed, according to newspaper reports, "would this kid, twenty years of age, do this to a police officer." They shouted that the officer must have been lying about what had happened. The dead man was initially thought to have been eighteen years of age, because he had been using his cousin's name to hide his own identity.

Chuck was not terribly shocked at the distortions in the newspaper reports. "Well, that is just how the media writes about us," he thought. What became most distressing to him, however, was that reporters began to visit his parents' and grandparents' homes in search of a story. The department had listed on their website the names and working hours of all officers patrolling each neighborhood of the city, and so reporters were able to direct the focus of their efforts at him. He was being followed by people in cars who, when he approached them to ask who they were and why they were watching him, turned out to be reporters. A woman with "a sexy voice" telephoned his mother and asked for Chuck by his first name in a manner that suggested an acquaintance with him. She then began to ask his mother questions about the shooting. When Chuck's mother became suspicious about the purpose of her questions, she acknowledged then that she was a reporter.

His grandmother had been battling leukemia and had gone home for her last days. A reporter called her at 10:00 one night and asked whether "Chuck was all right." As this appeared to upset and scare Chuck's grandmother, who feared that her grandson had been injured or killed, the woman identified herself as a reporter. "If you find out anything about how he is doing, call us back," she instructed, and hung up. A few days later, his grandmother's condition rapidly deteriorated and she died.

For a number of months after the shooting, the department expressed concern about having Chuck perform his normal work assignments. A lieutenant told him he was "too hot," while a sergeant told him that he probably would not be permitted on any special assignments for a while. Chuck felt these individuals were punishing him because of the shooting and thus must have believed he had done wrong.

When Chuck told me this, I interrupted him and expressed grave concern. It was, I told him, precisely those officers who were alarmed by fears of what would happen to them if they defended themselves, or worked in the manner they normally did, who became preoccupied and distracted, and placed themselves in grave danger by acting in hesitant or indecisive ways.

Chuck admitted that his concerns about how he was perceived by his department did affect his work. "I wouldn't want to admit it, but if I had been attacked during that period my reaction would have been delayed." Chuck told me he had seen a person acting in a suspicious manner that he would, under normal circumstances, have stopped to check out. "I did not stop and check it out. . . . I drove right by. . . . I told myself, 'If that's what I get for doing good police work . . . why should I go out and work so hard to protect people by getting bad guys? Why don't I do what some of the others [officers] do . . . sit and wait for calls and get paid the same?' " He felt bitter about what had happened to him.

However, Chuck reported that, following his work with me on this event and its aftermath, things began to return to their normal perspective. "I remembered that the primary reason . . . is I like putting bad guys in jail. . . . Some people may be in it to make people in the community feel good about cops. I'm not. . . . I'm in it to put assholes in jail."

In the aftermath of the shooting incident, Chuck's mother, who was having a difficult time adjusting to what had happened to her son, was offered the same support given him by his department. During her session with me, she let a secret "out of the bag." She told me that her son's Christmas present to her each year had been to collect and buy food for disadvantaged people in the same neighborhood he patrolled in. He believed in the importance of sharing with those less fortunate than himself. As "tough" or "macho" as his words above might appear to some, in reality he often acted to make the community feel good. This aspect of himself, as it is with many of good character, was embarrassing to him; he wished no recognition for doing what he thought was right. How tragic if, after members of the same community branded him a murderer, he lost the gift of giving by withdrawing in bitterness from his community.

Chuck reported that the county sheriff's investigators had found his actions to be legal and proper. He felt uncomfortable that the department had held a meeting to "figure out how to release the findings . . . to appease the community." This came at a time when he was just beginning to engage in the normal mental and observational vigilance that made him a skilled and competent police officer. I am left wondering what impact the message, "You're hot . . . you're probably not going to get some assignments for awhile" will have in the future upon Chuck's ability and readiness to respond to threatening conditions.

Attempts to make police officers more in tune with the community are not at issue here. I myself have worked to enhance community policing activities by police officers. I have observed millions of dollars spent to create partnerships with the communities that the police serve, with excellent results. Supervision and training have emphasized the need to treat citizens with dignity, professionalism, and respect for their individuality. Police officers have been empowered to be creative in developing solutions to community problems. These solutions can only better the quality of life in local communities and facilitate further partnerships with the police.

The concern I am raising involves the "pendulum swing" in policy and public expectations of police work that leads to a number of problems that are preventable and manageable. We should not seek less aggressive officers and deputies. We should want vigorous, competitive, "refuse-to-lose" individuals to assist our communities. In my mind, the officer whose story you have just read is one of those who truly give meaning to the term "America's finest."

The first swing that the pendulum of organizational changes in law enforcement has taken has been extreme, pushed by powerful forces. Likewise, what happens when the pendulum returns the other way will likely also be excessive, driven by the initial forces creating the change. In future "swings," there need to be changes based upon scientifically gathered data, not politics or personal beliefs.

While there do exist examples of dysfunction and impropriety in police departments today, the painting of a majority of police officers as insensitive, untrustworthy, or highly likely to violate people's civil rights is patently inaccurate. It also exhibits a tremendous ignorance of the day-to-day acts of heroism and honor performed by police officers everywhere.

In addition, blanket condemnation of the police may well threaten the very liberties that make such condemnation possible. The alienation of police from the public creates a dangerous vacuum in which criminality as well as extremist political, racial, and/or religious fanaticism is more likely to prosper.

Today's police officer expects to be punished for performing his or her work (Blum, 1998). In a national sample of police officers studied in research I performed for the International Union of Police Associations, 43.8 percent of police officers and deputy sheriffs in our country reported that the impact of police work upon them includes an expectation that they will be punished if they do their job. This expectation of punishment cannot help but develop into some degradation in how officers perform.

Many police officers have told me that they have begun to lessen the vigor with which criminals are hunted and apprehended. Many have described turning their backs to suspicious-looking persons and vehicles simply because they don't want the "flak" that comes today from doing police work. Any citizen who seeks to avoid the responsibility for violations that he or she has committed only has to complain that the officer was rude, abusive, or intimidating, and a prolonged investigation—often taking over a year—will ensue. Criminals now know that society's reactions to policing in this country are giving them more and more of an edge to enable them to successfully perpetrate crime against the innocent.

An effective and appropriate police system in this country will only be ensured when society decides to look below the surface of sensationalism in the media and become educated about the realities of police work. The educated public will recognize that there must be proper supervision of the officer by individuals who are promoted by virtue of a demonstrated ability to lead and inspire others—not because of their gender, ethnicity, or special influence. Supervision at its best is a mentoring and coaching; both roles can incorporate accountability and discipline where necessary. Command and executive personnel must be driven to provide excellence in their management of the agency, rather than being motivated by "turf protection," in which they seek to enhance their own position, sphere of influence, and controlled resources within the agency. Most importantly, there must be active, participatory community support for excellence in law enforcement that is based upon a realistic knowledge of what actions are necessary to protect society, and not a biased, broad-brush distortion of law enforcement based on incidents that are not representative of the field as a whole.

7. *Secret Wars and Secret Casualties*

The development of Citizen Academies has begun the process of familiarizing local citizens with the realities of police work, and thus including them in the police system. This is a very promising activity, and must be expanded to involve a much greater percentage of the public and legislative and governmental decision makers. The phenomenon of denial that I mentioned in Chapter One has allowed too much of the police experience to be hidden from the public, with the result that most citizens are uninformed consumers of police services.

Any condition or circumstance that strongly influences how police perform should, in my opinion, be of utmost interest to the public in its scrutiny of policing. One of the most commonly discussed factors—and perhaps the least understood—is the phenomenon of police work stress. The literature is replete (see for example, Kroes, 1976; Violanti, Vena, and Marshall, 1986; et al.) with references to the fact that police work is a stressful occupation. But what does that really mean, and how does it impact the public?

As noted earlier, what people do every day becomes familiar to them, and the brain perceives this repeated pattern of external environmental conditions and internal physiological, emotional, and mental activity as normalcy. Each time a police officer is about to contact some person or event (e.g., "check the welfare," unknown trouble, suspicious circumstance, 911 "hang up" telephone call), his or her brain undergoes a cascade of reactions known as the **stress response**. The stress response results in the entire physiology and psychology of the individual being immediately altered in anticipation of decisive physical action, whether or not that action occurs. After repeated encounters with stressful events, the police brain begins to react according to those emergency patterns, even when no actual emergency is occurring. In other words, the brain habituates either to repeated experiences of stressful encounters at work, or to one single critical event, so that further encounters will not be shocking or injurious to the individual's viability.

The day-to-day stresses of policing are such that they are likely to create tissue and organ changes in the bodies of those who serve. It is a relatively normal phenomenon in police officers, for example, to have multiple awakenings from sleep, stiffness or tightness in the muscles without prior trauma, gastrointestinal symptoms of distress, and episodes of irritability, impatience, or dysphoric mood. These are all logical reactions to the body's being exposed to a relatively constant release of adrenaline, noradrenaline, and cortisol, the body's stress hormones, which are used to fuel an individual's alarm and "fight or flight" response. These reactions can also have a strong influence upon how the officer subsequently performs his or her duties. Since the brain is also a target organ of stress, officers' minds, moods, thoughts, and judgments can be expected to be negatively impacted over time as a direct result of stressful conditions that are inescapable in their work (Blum, 1998; 2000).

"Shut Up and Take the Pain"

"We were originally designated as a perimeter or cover team . . . but the way it happened, everybody became a cover team. There was a helicopter. The house was by a freeway, so no officer even heard the shots when Tony was killed," Mike told me.

Mike and Tony were part of a multi-agency narcotics task force that was performing a reverse sting, an undercover operation in which a police investigator poses as a drug dealer and arrests the crooks who buy the drugs. Tony was on a different agency's crew, but he had worked successfully with Mike's crew on a number of cases. On this one, though, there were a number of danger signals or "red flags" that something was wrong. Tony had approached Mike's crew where they were seated in the briefing room, looked directly at them, and said, "If this thing goes bad, I'll be fighting for my life. I need you guys to get there." "Don't worry," Mike and the other three guys from their crew assured him, "we have your back." Mike and his crew meant what they said to Tony. They were a close-knit group of narcotics officers. The events of that day have haunted them since 1991, when they were unable to keep their promise to Tony.

Tony had called the crook's house from a pay phone a couple of blocks away and was told that he could not bring his partner into the house with him. "Right then it should have stopped, but we didn't. It was a big case, you know," Mike told me. It was clear that such hindsight was a source of pain to him even years later.

There were thirty-nine police officers and helicopters involved in the direct operation, with several more police resources deployed as a backup. When the crooks unexpectedly changed the plan, Tony couldn't tell the cover officers, who were a half-block away, where he would be. "We were blocked by the freeway overpass from seeing the kill zone. The fact that there was a plan but that all of a sudden we did not know where Tony was going was more troubling than not having any plan at all," Mike told me. "When the 998 [emergency code the police use to communicate that shots have been fired, and an officer is in need of immediate help] came out, everybody ran in. Then they heard the helicopter put out on the radio that multiple suspects were running from the rear of the house with guns. When I got there, guys were just standing there in shock . . . standing around Tony. I knew he was dead. Blood was still pouring out of him, but you could tell he was dead."

Mike and the other officers did the only thing that they could at this point. "We went in pursuit," he told me. "The helicopter was putting out the locations of the suspects. I was in my unit. When I turned a corner on the next street west, I observed a suspect matching the description of the shooters walking down the street towards me. I slammed on my brakes and jumped out of the car and prone him. He complied with everything. This was the guy who shot Tony in the back . . . who was also wanted for another homicide," he said. It took everything Mike had to follow the rules and stop himself from pummeling or shooting this suspect for the murder of his buddy and partner. They took the suspect into custody. Several witnesses called out to the officers that they had seen two Hispanic males running into the church.

As Mike started to tell me what had happened in the church, he appeared physically as well as mentally oppressed by the memory. With difficulty, he told me that several officers had refused to go into the church with him and Ernie, the investigator from his crew who had told Tony not to worry, that they had his back. "This was a rapidly fluid case," he told me. "There was no time to do a tactical containment and perimeter. It was one of those times you just had to risk your ass. Ernie and I made entry. Ernie went upstairs and I went into the main sanctuary. The church was housed in a converted commercial building. It had no windows to the outside. It was pitch black inside the church. We screamed at the pastor and his wife to get out, and then we didn't know where the lights were. Ernie and I were separate and alone, looking for two Hispanic males who had just murdered a police officer."

In the movie *Black Hawk Down*, there is a scene in which the Delta Force and SEAL forces prepare for their raid into Mogadishu, Somalia. They neglect to bring extra water, ammunition, bulletproof vests, or food, because the raid is just supposed to be a half-hour "jaunt" into Mogadishu. When even the most elite forces in the world can prejudge and mistake a situation so completely, it should not be surprising that these officers had not fully equipped themselves on this operation, a decision that was to be life-altering in Mike's case.

"I'm in the dark searching alone. . . . We didn't have flashlights because it was a daytime operation. . . . The radio traffic comes out that the helicopter is landing at the crime scene to get Tony. The way the traffic came out, I knew Tony was dead, and I was committed to trying to stay alive. I came in from a bright June day into the darkness. I couldn't see my hand in front of my face."

"I was on my hands and knees, and felt around with my hand in front of me so I was sure I wouldn't miss someone that would kill another cop. I was searching chair to chair, praying that I would fire first if something happened. If I got into a firefight the muzzle flash of the gun would have blinded me anyway. . . . After that, we searched the adjacent building, and then the local agency and the world started showing up and relieved us."

As he drove back to the local police department to meet all the officers who were involved in this case, the surge of hormones that had created such a high level of vigilance and emotional and physical arousal began to ebb. "The adrenaline had worn off by then, and the reality of what had just happened hit me," Mike told me. "I sagged. I felt on the verge of collapse. I'd been pumping so hard. When we got to the station, we saw the suspects being walked in front of us into the detention area behind the station. This was extremely difficult."

As Mike had arrested one of the shooters, he was interviewed for a long time by investigating detectives, and then "drove home by myself in the dark. [I know now that] that shouldn't have happened, given what happened to me later."

"I felt totally alone. . . . There were the other guys in groups huddled together, hysterically crying, and I had never felt more alone. So I isolated [myself] and shoved it down for all I was worth. In my whole life, shoving it down had always worked," he said. "It didn't work this time."

149

As he was driving back to his home department in the aftermath of this shocking and tragic event, he was struck again by the feeling he had had in the church. He told no one that he was unable to conquer the feelings of hyper-vigilance, fear, and impending violence and harm that had overwhelmed him when he was blinded by the darkness, searching for Tony's killer. Indeed, Mike cannot fall asleep to this day (eleven years later) unless there is a light on somewhere in his purview.

"When I came to see you that day, Doc," Mike told me, "I didn't feel I had the right to be devastated like this because I wasn't as personally close with Tony as the other guys were. So I literally sat in a chair in my dining room for several days and kept everybody away . . . maybe it would go away. I kept my family away . . . huge mistake."

Thus began the alteration in Mike's personality, social relationships, and work performance that would take away all that he had worked for. Unfortunately, by the time Mike decided to unload the painful and destructive "internal baggage" that he carried around with him, the wounds he bore, though possessing no entry mark or scar that could be pointed to, had drastically altered his life.

Mike's war has been a secret one, and his wounds were always kept secret as well. Like almost all police officers, Mike tried to "shove [his feelings] down" in an attempt to cope with the stresses of his work without doing anything that would permit other officers to perceive them as weak. The message to them is clear from the first day of the Academy: "Shut up and take the pain."

Whether a police officer encounters violent felons or the day-to-day frustrations of taking calls for service from unhappy citizens, the effects of the body's response to stress will result in unavoidable alterations in that officer's mood, thoughts, judgment, and emotional reactions. Without training, mentoring, and assistance in managing and controlling their internal physical, mental, and emotional reactions to work stress—resources that are a part of stress exposure training and are currently underutilized—police officers' work performance as well as their health will likely suffer accordingly.

As discussed in *Force under Pressure: How Cops Live and Why They Die*, we have learned methods that enable officers to control their internal physiological and psychological reactions under conditions of stress. We have applied these methods successfully to tactical training for police officers, and they have proven capable of preventing perceptual distortion and shock reactions during unanticipated and/or uncontrolled threat. The task now is for police officers to be provided with such training and resources.

Those Left Behind

There are memorial services held each year for officers and deputies who are killed in the line of duty. Each state honors its dead each year, and there is a national memorial service in Washington, D.C. I was speaking at the California memorial one year at the request of two people. One was the father of a young Highway Patrol Officer who had been murdered. The father had retired from a long and distinguished career in the same department. The other was the wife of a murdered deputy sheriff. Both police persons had been killed while in the performance of their duties.

Both father and wife are quite active and involved in a group called Concerns of Police Survivors (COPS). COPS provides a peer support network for the survivors of police officers and deputies killed on duty. It responds immediately to the family of the murdered officer and offers assistance and aid. The slain deputy's wife often jokes at the talks she gives to police officers since her election as the national President of COPS: "We're the only group that doesn't want their membership to grow."

At the meeting I attended, the room was filled with children, adults, and senior citizens, all members of a terrible fraternity—their loved ones had been torn from them through violent death while in the service of the community. I had seen too many of them before.

The murder of police officers causes hundreds of casualties across the country every year, but this fact does not appear to have been of sufficient notoriety for the media to make much of it. Police officers and their families have experienced the same grief and loss as the World Trade Center victims and their families. Perhaps society will now broaden the scope of its support and compassion of the heroes and victims of September 11 to include those who have given their lives in more secret wars.

A short time after the murder of one of its officers or deputies, the department, like everyone else in the world, goes back to "business." Survivors cling to the promises once made to them that they were joining a family, but many are treated as a reminder of sad events and are made aware that they make others uncomfortable. Groups like COPS advocate for the survivors years afterward. They also use their terrible knowledge to provide support to new victims by pairing them with a person who has lived through a similar experience. A woman who lost her husband to violence while she was pregnant with their child will respond to a pregnant wife whose husband is killed, or a father whose daughter or son was killed will talk to the parents of a murdered officer.

Play by the Rules and Pay the Price
While it might be surprising to some, the type of circumstance that results in the most frequent post-traumatic stress reaction is not a violent incident, such as hand-to-hand combat or an officer-involved shooting. While violent contacts certainly result in lifelong physical, mental, emotional, interpersonal, and social consequences for many police officers, contact with child victims is the most commonly reported source of post-traumatic stress reactions by a national sample of police officers (Blum, 1998).

Kelly, a detective assigned to crimes against children, was more surprised than anything else when she collapsed. She had been unaware that anything was happening to her. Her focus of attention had always been on the victim. "The victims had already been hurt so badly. . . . I wanted to ease them through the system, to take care of them. . . . The parents couldn't help. . . . Sometimes they were the suspects . . . the victim's family was torn apart or [they were] evil."

She was unconcerned with her own well-being. In this sense, Kelly was like most of the good members of law enforcement. However, all of the detectives in her unit were overwhelmed with caseload responsibilities. "One case I worked . . . I found eleven more victims. I wound up with thirty-two other cases on my desk because my supervisor never took off the pressure. Management ignored [our] well-being . . . no gap between horrific cases. . . ."

It saddens me that, while the public's sympathy and grief pours out for nationally reported tragedies such as the murders of Polly Klaas and Samantha Runnion, most are unaware that cops like Kelly live in this horrible world every single day of their careers.

Kelly began to feel as if what was happening to her was separating her from the realities of life. When she was not on duty she was a mother and a wife. She and her husband were raising three children. She began to feel as if the rest of her family lived in one world while she moved through another—a world of sexual molestation, sexual assault, physical abuse, and homicide, all perpetrated against children.

To protect the victim, she had to build a case—get the criminal and bring him or her to justice. She had to interview the victim (if living), as well as witnesses and suspects. She would determine the existence of any other cases involving this suspect through records kept by the Child Protective Services agency in her city.

I had known of Kelly's reputation as an expert detective and interviewer through classes I taught to police detectives. During my interview with her I commented that she used precisely the strategies that I attempt to teach (basing one's questions upon the behavioral characteristics of the perpetrator as opposed to a "just the facts, ma'am" approach). Her face lit up: "The fact that I'm a female helped. . . . I exploited their 'macho' contempt of women. . . . They would talk to me . . . nailing their coffin. . . . My interview strategies put bad people in prisons. . . . Some people just need to be locked away, and it is possible to do that by the rules."

I told Kelly that it was my experience that police officers, deputies, and investigators who play by the rules pay a price. A piece of themselves is sacrificed in order to perform with the excellence they demonstrate as individuals. She gave me permission to divulge that she had collapsed while at work, a short number of months after her partner, another female, had been forced off work by life-threatening heart episodes. This was in fact Kelly's second collapse, but she had been successful in keeping the first episode a secret.

"The males in my unit were not assigned as many cases as [she and her partner] got," she told me. "I didn't understand why." When I spoke to her sergeant, he acknowledged the truth of her statement. He said that he assigned a greater number of cases to her and her female partner because they would "handle it in ways the men wouldn't."

Some supervisors and "worker bee" police personnel are concerned with "closing" cases. This detective's concern was building a "rock-solid case that would last for the rest of their [the victim's] life. . . .You do everything possible to lessen their pain while ignoring yours."

Kelly had nothing physically wrong with her. However, she had become another casualty amid the sea of children's faces that flooded her mind—children who had been raped, molested, abused, and murdered. She became depressed to the point that she could no longer work. After two very difficult years of treatment, she was successful in returning herself to health, thanks in large measure to her religious beliefs. She no longer walks through the world as if wearing dark glasses that prevent her from seeing color and light. Unfortunately, there are many examples of casualties in secret wars of law enforcement that do not end as happily.

Deep undercover assignments are another little-recognized source of police casualties. Mike, the surviving partner in the

Narcotics Enforcement operation described above, was approached in 1996 by a police commander who was in charge of developing a major "sting" operation together with the Secret Service, Department of Alcohol, Tobacco, and Firearms, business corporations, and local police agencies. The commander gave Mike the opportunity to work a deep undercover sting operation to buy stolen property in Los Angeles and Orange counties. This was a top-secret and complex operation. No one other than Mike's chief and commanding officer could know the details of the assignment. He was told to "go home and think about it," because he was being asked for total commitment for at least one year. Mike had been working and living with the expectation that his undercover days were over. He perceived the chance to "do it again" as a divine intervention.

He had no illusions. He had seen Tony murdered in front of him while working undercover. He perceived the new assignment as the ultimate test of his abilities—to be turned loose on L.A. crime. He was put on thirty days of leave to "put his things in order" and clean out his desk. He met with the commander at the storefront where they would work. The Secret Service people were there. He got equipment and a safe house, and construction was done to the storefront to authenticate its appearance as a front for a "fence" of stolen property.

Mike opened for business in March of 1996. They made up a flyer ("We buy jewelry, cell phones, etc.") and taped them on telephone poles in neighborhoods containing gang activity and high crime. "The crooks were lined up at the door. . . . I never had one honest person call in one year to sell legitimate goods. . . . All of it was crooked. . . . One was a medical student at U.C.L.A. who had tapped into public long distance telephone lines . . . but mostly killers."

He started out working the storefront, but was quickly forced to change the original plan, as the crooks did not want to continue coming to the store, often asking him to visit "chop shops" to view the stolen car parts they were selling. In addition to the chop shop auto and parts theft ring, he worked cases dealing in telephone fraud and stolen phones, stolen electronic equipment, stolen jewelry, and a goodly amount of heroin sold to him by the crooks. He marked each visit on video, and noted each in a case log in the store. He also took notes in the field.

One difficulty he faced was that, while he had to stay "in character" with highly sophisticated criminals, he also had to maintain his safety—not an easy task under these conditions—and be able to identify the suspects later on during prosecution. He went to the home turf of Crips, Bloods, and Pirus (three notorious criminal gangs in Los Angeles area). "It was a very scary place—no radio, no backup. . . . No one knew my location . . . totally surrounded, totally outgunned." They would blindfold him and take him, circling in their vehicles to disorient him. "Any second could be your last . . . just like the Alamo . . . no one coming to your rescue."

Over and over again, day after day, he worked undercover in these conditions. No relief was provided him, as he was responsible as lead agent for any partner assigned to him. "No one monitoring you . . . you start to lose touch. At times I felt uninvolved, at other times like death. . . . At the same time I was raising a family."

He would go from living in insanity, being someone else entirely, to trying to be normal at home while the bad guys were calling him on the phone to bail them out of jail. He would be speaking on the phone with his "crook buddies" on the way to his son's athletic games. He could not divulge the details of his work to his wife: "Even if I could, what would I say? The whole family was falling apart."

He had to become friends with the crooks, so that they would bring others to the store. "You have to maintain your relationships, like any business, except this is with crooks. In doing so, you totally lose any sense of officer safety, [police] procedures; the actions that are necessary in undercover work go against everything learned as a police officer. You must give up all hope of getting out of it. . . . You have to show you're nuts so many times [in order to present a tough demeanor to the crooks], you eventually lose the fear that people use for caution . . . no contact with the police other than going over accounting with the lieutenant once every couple of weeks. You'd occasionally risk your life by going to the station. . . . I felt alienated there, as if no one knew who I was anymore. You don't even know you're lost . . . you're so lost. . . . "

At the end of the project, seventy felony indictments were filed against fifty major criminals in the area. Mike was not permitted to make the transition back to his agency. His department provided no transitional support or counseling, a basic and fundamental agency response with any field officer in any undercover operation.

The person he had been prior to the sting project was gone. He and his wife separated. He and his department separated. He has kept his relationship with his son and his God; that is what he has left to him. He was not recognized for his heroism by his department or municipality. He was, however, left with episodes of fear, anxiety, rage, amnesia, mental disorientation, tachycardia, and a sense of betrayal and abandonment by the very people he gave his life to serve.

For many police officers, the donning of their uniform, body armor, and the image projected to the world serves to form a protective shield against a bombardment of frustration, pain, and suffering that they will encounter on a daily basis. And yet, many officers do not survive. Some are shot down by an assailant's bullet. Others are killed, maimed, or crippled in traffic collisions. Others die of heart attacks, liver damage, kidney failure, or strokes. Some police officers take their own lives in the throes of anger, hurt, and helplessness. Still others do not last the twenty to thirty years needed for a service retirement. They are injured, either physically or psychologically. The list of stories of wounded men and women in police work could fill several books such as this. It is time for society to better get to know the secret wars and secret casualties of law enforcement, so that the public will be better able to pressure the right people to do the right things for excellence in law enforcement and in the community.

8. What It Takes to Do It Right

I have been most fortunate to observe the epitome of excellence in police work over the past twenty years of service as a police psychologist. I have been witness to the worst in law enforcement as well. Acts of heroism and cowardice have defined opposite ends of a continuum of courage and honor in police work.

One can observe similarities in the characteristics of those police agencies whose work is defined by excellence, honor, compassion, and heroism. Conversely, it is not difficult to observe consistent themes in police agencies whose officers have faltered in these four areas.

It never ceases to amaze me that, in all the hue and cry of such incidents as the Rampart scandal in Los Angeles and the Abner Louima violation in New York, there was no mention of the supervision and command that were supposed to guide, direct, and manage the actions of the police. The actions allegedly undertaken by Rafael Perez with a small number of thugs were said to have occurred over a prolonged period of time and over scores of criminal cases. Where was the focus of attention of supervisory responsibility directed during this time? Why were these individuals not held accountable on a daily basis for negligence or malfeasance in their work? Is it more practical to scrutinize the line officer only? I do not believe that the actions of line police officers can be viewed separately from their position in a structured system where each component exerts influence upon how the police officers in that organization perform their work.

Police corruption can only occur within a vacuum of leadership and a lack of supervisory accountability. It feeds off the *laissez faire* and "cover your ass" sensibilities that may characterize the leadership, ignoring many important departmental issues that require attention.

The quality of a police department and the excellence in its officers' or deputies' performance will, in large measure, be influenced by the actions of its leadership. Because of the military rank structure within police agencies, the chief's words are law, and his or her vision guides and drives the department to its destiny. His or her presence—or lack thereof—in the pursuit of excellence and doing "the right thing" will determine the extent of accountability worn by all within the department.

To do what is right, the leadership of police agencies must be visible, present, and involved in the daily operations of the department, making all accountable by a continual monitoring and drive towards excellence even as the leaders themselves are responsible for relationships with the outside community and city or county government. To whatever extent alienation exists between components of a police agency, to that extent the seeds of potential for performance corruption are sown.

Police Leadership and Organizational Guidance

> *"The best leaders the people hardly know*
> *The next best they love and praise*
> *The next they fear*
> *And the next they hate"*
> (Dao de Jing or The Way of Power)

The above quote by the sage Lao Zi does a good job of representing the impact of styles and types of leadership on those who follow. In another section of the *Dao de Jing*, Lao Zi writes, "I have three treasures to be maintained and cherished: The first is love; the second is frugality; the third is not pushing oneself ahead of others. From love comes courage; from frugality comes generosity; from not pushing oneself ahead of others comes leadership."

The verb "to lead" means "showing the way to or directing the course of; to conduct; or to guide" (Webster's New World Dictionary, Second College Edition, 1984). A leader is one who leads, commands, or guides, as the head of a group or activity. An ethical leader commands or guides others to acts of goodness. While there is a myriad of types, styles, and actions that characterize police leadership in this country, all such leaders are responsible for commanding and guiding others to acts of goodness within the purview of law enforcement.

As noted in a previous chapter, the chief executive officer of a police organization observes the world through a "multi-paned window." Very few outside of police organizations can comprehend the immensity of the political, social, media, and organizational pressures and stresses encountered daily by chief executive officers in law enforcement. It is just not feasible to think that such pressures are not going to affect the decisions that the leader must make.

The ability to effectively and properly balance the often competing forces of virtue and pragmatism does exist in a large number of police organizations, and is demonstrated by a number of current leaders in the field of law enforcement. With little in the way of public fame, these individuals have effected the creation of healthy, vibrant, community-responsive, creative, and proactive police agencies.

In these organizations, the same leader who disciplines an officer for policy violation will comfort that officer without grudge or malice. I was once called to a police department at 2:45 a.m. following an officer-involved shooting. A police officer had attempted to take an individual into custody. When the officer approached, the subject ran down the alley he had been seen in front of. When the officer followed him in pursuit, he turned and fired a gun at him. The Watch Commander told me that the officer seemed okay but shaken up by the incident. I arrived at the department at 3:50 a.m. and was directed to the officer. When I entered the room, I saw his chief, G. "Steve" Simonian, who was known for being a tough disciplinarian, sitting with his arms around the officer, comforting him.

The chief of police will protect the citizens of his or her community by enforcing excellence, honor, integrity, and professionalism in his or her troops—and accepts nothing less. At the same time, he or she will show great care and concern for the quality of life and well-being of his or her employees, providing the training, resources, and work environment that are necessary for the achievement of excellence.

A drive for integrity, honor, and excellence; equity in holding all employees accountable for their actions; great care and concern for the skill development, quality of life, and well-being of their members; and outreach to the community are consistently observed signs that a police agency's leadership is doing what is right.

The extent to which the commanders of the police agency support the leader's vision in the performance of their duties will also have a great deal of influence upon the quality of police services therein. From an organizational perspective, what is required to do what is right is a departmental apparatus in which employees in each component of the system, from Records Clerks through the chief executive officer, work to support officers in their work with the utmost integrity, moral responsibility, and ethics. This means the supervisory and command staff must perceive themselves as enhancers and facilitators of the work of their personnel, and not be primarily concerned about self-defense or self-aggrandizement. A fragmented command staff, or one with insufficient skill or experience necessary to command, will undo the efforts of a well-intentioned leader who is not willing to take control of the agency or to make firm decisions and commands. There are many police executives who are under so much pressure that their energies are primarily spent on getting through each day unscathed. These are the agencies in which problems are likely to occur due to a vacuum of leadership.

The leadership of police agencies must be able and willing to make the tough decisions that enable effective resolution to organizational problems. This means they must contend with severe and prolonged pressure and stress. The physical and emotional health and well-being of police executives must be supported and maintained by a rigorous approach to work fitness (see Work Fitness, below). Such is not now the case. I have spent a number of years speaking before chiefs' and sheriffs' associations in several California counties, and have been struck by the consistency with which these executives suffer from hypertension, gastrointestinal disorders, depression, anxiety, and premonitions of threat. When the chief executive is buckling under the pressure of leadership, a vacuum is created that will likely be filled by others who lack or disagree with the chief's vision and values.

A number of chief executive officers were interviewed for this book to ascertain their views and positions on leadership, training, values, and police performance. They were selected because they represent different-sized, highly functional and professional police agencies whose relationships with their communities of service are vibrant and viable. The morale in their departments is high, and employees perform their duties with pride. (Notable among these are Sheriffs Bill Kolender and Leroy Baca of the San Diego County and Los Angeles County Sheriff's Departments, respectively, Joe Polisar of the Garden Grove Police Department, Randy Narramore of the Huntington Park Police Department, and G. "Steve" Simonian, Los Angeles County District Attorney's Bureau of Investigation.)

All were faced at the beginning with whatever challenges their predecessors had left behind. There was a high level of consistency in the steps they took in assuming the stewardship of large, urban sheriff's departments and small to moderate-sized police departments. They took a stance of inclusion in the organizational decision-making process with their employees that altered the dynamics of the organization immediately.

Instead of laying out their personal views of how police work had to be done for all to follow, they began a process of needs assessment with their employees. They asked people from each component of the organization, both sworn officers and civilian employees in all divisions, how their job needed to be done to be at its most excellent. They asked their employees what they needed to be trained in to become expert in their area of work. They asked what employees needed in the way of facilities, resources, and equipment to get the job done properly. A well-functioning police department must perform its tasks according to the best scientific knowledge and information available, using the equipment, resources, and support necessary to create success. While this feature of policing may be taken for granted, the fact remains that many police departments in this country have either outdated or, at times, insufficient equipment with which to perform highly difficult and dangerous assignments.

From the rank of captain on up (and, in smaller departments, lieutenant), all command staff were assigned the task of developing the agency's vision, mission, and values—values within the community and within the department. "Meaningful change comes from within the organization and the individual. You make it meaningful for each . . . in the organization and make it their job to give ideas. . . . [T]he issue . . . is leadership, so commanders and chiefs don't feel entitlement, but, rather, accountability. . . . Society thinks a cop shoots someone and goes to lunch. The reality is we must give psychological care [to the involved deputies or officers]" (Kolender, 2001).

Sheriff Kolender spent a good deal of his initial months in office giving classes to each and every employee of the department in the mission and code of ethics for which they would be accountable. In addition, he expended a substantial amount of energy educating and interacting with elected officials to increase understanding and support for the department.

When he was elected Sheriff of Los Angeles County, Leroy Baca visited each one of the seventy commands he led in order to evaluate the health of the department, its cultures, its actual performance— "and what it should be" (Baca, 2001). Baca believes in the importance of maximizing the individual potential of his employees, and does all that is necessary to ensure that each employee uses innovation and leadership in the performance of his or her duties. He has extended and broadened the role of deputy sheriff in his agency.

Sheriff Baca believes that decision making and problem solving cannot wait for executive review. He trusts and empowers his field supervisors and commanders to make the immediate tactical decisions: "[The] modern deputy in [the] Los Angeles County Sheriff's Department will understand common sense, and fairness will guide the department's response to force. The only time you worry about who's in charge is when things are messed up. You need to provide persistent leadership. Deputies don't let things slide, but the role for deputy is now expanded to outreach, counseling, in addition to their task to go get those who are not involved in the democratic process" (Baca, 2001).

Bill Stonich, the Undersheriff of the Los Angeles County Sheriff's Department, is struck by the change in the role of deputy sheriff that has evolved over the years. For example, when he first became a deputy thirty-two years ago, his father, an Illinois State Trooper, advised him about responding to a family fight call (the single most dangerous type of contact for police officers in terms of injuries incurred): "Get in, get out, and don't get drawn into taking sides ..."

Sheriff Stonich noted that society now demands more than name-takers. "We in law enforcement have obligations to arrest the perpetrator, to prosecute, and . . . to protect the victim, even when the victim denies the need for protection." He noted that for twenty-nine of the thirty-two years he has spent in law enforcement, he felt that his obligation was to seek out and arrest law violators. He never gave thought to rehabilitation of law violators, or secondary prevention through Community Outreach programs.

"Intervention [by deputies] is very recent. . . . Lee Baca says, 'You're a social worker' . . . involved in the community. We run the single largest rehabilitation program [in custody facilities] in Biscailuz Recovery Center, deputies and 'treaters' interacting with abusers of drugs, alcohol . . . people . . . in [an] effort to change behavior."

The conversion of the Biscailuz jail facility into a combined custody and treatment center is quite a remarkable innovation. Commanders and supervisors within the ranks of the department who were initially aghast at the thought of broadening the scope of the custody function found themselves becoming proponents of an intervention that was working to lessen the recidivism of men who abused people and chemicals. A number of former inmates returned for a recent graduation ceremony, because they wanted to feel proud at completing the change.

The facility was the pride of the Sheriff's Department: "[The] Los Angeles Sheriff's Department has pride that we're the best, in embracing the changes that society demanded made" (Stonich, 2002).

Sheriff Baca noted that the more you invest in leadership, self-management, and team building, the more results will be achieved. However, he noted a concern I found profound and relevant to all types of law enforcement efforts: "The biggest secret is not the Code of Silence [the term used to describe the widely perceived pattern of officers covering for another officer's wrongdoing]. It's getting cops to tell you that they're in over their heads." He stated that his officers are good people with strong moral and ethical values, but are forced to confront situations that may quickly result in their being overwhelmed. He feels strongly that a leader should not let "amateur" evaluators supplant his or her understanding of what occurs in the reality (as opposed to theory) of police work, even as he or she integrates the values that external forces introduce to the agency.

Court Orders, Consent Decrees, and Social Demand

Court orders and Federal Consent Decrees have been imposed upon police agencies to balance the department's ethnic membership in the same proportion as the community outside, to alter promotions so that a required percentage of women fill different ranks, and to change complaint and discipline procedures performed within the agency.

Departmental Use of Force policies have been scrutinized as well to ensure fairness, respect for the dignity and rights of citizens in contact with the police, and minimal use of force by the police. Such pressures for change upon police organizations, which are usually resistant to change, appear likely to improve law enforcement in a number of ways. However, there are significant problems and dilemmas facing law enforcement today as these good changes are brought in.

First, in terms of hiring: I do not believe that deficits in life experience (e.g., independent living, paying one's own bills, managing finances, holding jobs) should keep one from employment in law enforcement, as the job will certainly provide such experience and more. Given the characteristics of many in today's applicant pool for law enforcement, my concern is that mentoring programs in social adjustment, and specific training and practice in critical thinking under conditions of adversity (especially interpersonal adversity), should be an emphasized addition to the early educational content provided in police academies, and in the field training curriculum provided to police recruits. As noted earlier, this book's contention is that, after character, integrity, and honor, the single most important attribute/skill for the success of police action by today's officer or deputy is critical decision making under stress. Today's applicant pool (sarcastically referred to as the "Nintendo generation" by Academy instructors) cannot always be depended upon to be capable of making a critical decision and acting decisively, unemotionally, and in a self-disciplined, self-controlled manner under stressful conditions, without specific training, mentoring, and supervision to assist them in developing the necessary skills. We should not assume that police recruits possess these inherent attributes and abilities. They should be practicing and demonstrating such skills and habits over and over again under supervision.

It just does not make sense to emphasize diversity and community involvement within police agencies, and then assign unprepared individuals to responsible duties that, as Sheriff Baca points out above, can place them in a situation they aren't equipped to cope with.

Supportive changes in how Academy training is performed should be considered to increase recruits' skill, knowledge, and preparedness to confront all circumstances with the same ability and aplomb. The current emphasis upon tactical communication, service-oriented policing, and fitness/survival is necessary and appropriate. However, we must, I believe, accept the facts of life about generational changes in police applicants over time, and adapt teaching emphases to integrate those changes into law enforcement training so that knowledge, attitudes, and values can be successfully transferred from instructor to trainee. This could be done, for example, by creating a mentoring relationship wherein supervisors would continue to train, supervise, guide, and monitor newer officers. Mentoring provides a critical social adjustment support for recruits who may have very limited life experience. It can also provide the individual recognition that many of today's young adults crave for their efforts, in contrast to the group orientation observed in past generations.

Another concern arising from attempts at reform involves scrutiny, social prejudice, and the use of force: Any time a police use of force occurs, the leadership of the department is tasked to identify the possible economic and political liability for the department, the municipality, and the individuals staffing those leadership and municipal positions. Greater scrutiny, criticism, and scandals, coupled with lessened community support, have resulted in many cops becoming cynical and in danger of forgetting the purpose and mission of their work.

Other officers have become more reticent about using physical control as a tool or resource with disturbing, disturbed, resistant, or assaultive persons. Entering police recruits, anxious to earn the trust of the community, often abandon tactical tools in an attempt to maintain verbal contact with a person. Many also report a complete lack of experience with physical conflict when I interview them prior to their employment. Aggression as a resource and tool for police officers is becoming an endangered species. I take this issue somewhat personally, as I have been touched by the people who are left behind when their spouse or loved one is murdered in the line of duty—an officer who was likely looking for the good in the very person who killed him or her.

The general response tendency I have observed in police organizations when concerns arise about uses of force is an increase in policy limitations and a clarification of policy statements and of the rules of engagement that officers are to use. This alone is an unhelpful strategy, because added rules and more extensive risk management via policy do nothing to increase officers' ability to respond properly under stressful conditions.

As I have said before, aggression is not a dirty word. It is the source of a successful defense against predators who continue to exist and plague communities regardless of the debates occurring in city and academic chambers. Aggression is required to save the lives of the innocent that are threatened by the guilty. It is a force for and of life. Yes, it can be and has been used inappropriately. However, the vast majority of officers who have engaged in controversial actions did not do so because they were mean or bad. They were mentally or emotionally unprepared for the encounter, or lacked sufficient resources to control the threat.

Many police academies have changed their policies to allow individuals a chance to learn without the stress or adversity that was traditionally applied via a military boot camp model. For example, if an individual in one of these academies is having difficulty in a role-playing problem that involves intense emotions being discharged, he or she will not, as was done in the past, be berated or criticized for resting, or be denied a second or even a third chance to cope with the problem after a period of adjustment. This is a mistaken approach, because these officers will not be given the opportunity to "take five" in the field, and are being inadequately prepared to defend themselves and others. Another problem is that very few academies teach hand-to-hand grappling and sparring, which involves the exchange of blows or ground-fighting. For whatever reason, usually a risk management effort to avoid costs associated with inadvertent injury, or because such action goes against the model of policing being sought in that Academy, these physical, survival-oriented tools are neglected. This neglect will more than likely result in officers' or deputies' failure to adapt successfully to physical assaults against them. Officers who lack skills and confidence in hand-to-hand physical combat are more likely to attempt to use greater force than would otherwise have been necessary. The other possibility when an officer is insufficiently prepared for a physical assault is that he or she will be killed.

The problem as I perceive it is that the reality of police contacts is not black-and-white, predictable, or orderly. Their proper handling requires that an individual assess the situation and make the correct decision in a severe compression of time—with, at times, lethal consequences for error or delay.

It is a grave error, I believe, to seek the elimination of aggression in police officers. Everything that is known about the science of tactics points to the need to seize or gain, and then maintain, the initiative in a confrontation intended to impose the will of the commander or officer upon the criminal or disordered person. Once it is established that, because of a suspect's actions, verbal tools are not viable, then the proper action is an aggressive police response—not hesitancy, indecision, or continuing to give verbal commands well after the commands have become irrelevant.

Police officers often have to engage in decision making under conditions of stress. Because of concern on the part of an officer or deputy about limitations on the use of force identified in policy statements; and because of fiscal constraints upon Academy and Field Training, Academy curriculum and advanced officer training must use a methodology consistent with stress exposure training (see for example Cannon-Bowers and Salas, 1998; Kozlowski, 1998). Adult education methods prepare the individual well as long as he or she can accurately recognize what procedures an incident in the here and now requires, and has practiced the necessary skills sufficiently. They do not prepare the individual for unanticipated circumstances or rapidly changing or chaotic conditions. For that, the best science has documented that the training must include at least moderate degrees of adversity to facilitate effective and accurate decision making under stressful conditions (Cannon-Bowers and Salas, 1998).

Stress Exposure Training

The psychology of policing has little to do with emotions and moods. It has to do with ensuring that those performing police duties make

171

a proper assessment of some event, using analytical thought rather than instinctive or impulsive reactions. They must base their assessment upon the events that are occurring in their presence, and not allow their analysis to be influenced by their own personality, attitudes, or predilections.

Having made the proper assessment of a situation, police officers must then decide what resources will be required and what actions they will need to take. Again, they must not permit any preoccupations or distractions to delay or influence their decision. Given that their assessments and decisions are accurate and proper, they then must perform the appropriate action at a suitable rate, and with the proper degree of influence or, where necessary, force. Normally, they must perform these tasks under conditions of adversity, e.g., time compression, threat, risk, or unknown, confusing, or incomplete information.

In order to perform these tasks properly, police officers need to become experienced with the principles and practices presented in the discussion on stress exposure training presented in Chapter Four (see Training for Maximal Performance). They must become experts on the stress response, know what types of events are likely to trigger stress reactions within themselves, and demonstrate adaptive expertise in engaging in those methods that will prevent any disruption, dysfunction, or impropriety in their performance under stressful conditions. This expertise is not now developed in police officers, and in my opinion this deficit in their preparation predisposes them to experience degradation in their performance during critical events—those that contain unanticipated threat, rapidly changing conditions, and/or chaos. It just does not make sense for society to raise such outcry when a police officer is seen on a videotape slamming a handcuffed person on the hood of a car and punching him (KABC-TV, Los Angeles, July 6, 2002), without also demanding that police officers be much better prepared to deal with

172

adverse conditions without resorting to actions that are so disturbing to the public eye.

A closer look at stress exposure training may be helpful here. There are three primary objectives of stress exposure: 1) gaining knowledge of, and familiarity with, the reactions of the brain and body under stress; 2) training in skill acquisition required to maintain effective performance under stress; and 3) building confidence in performance through mastery learning. Peak performance is a difficult goal to attain under the best of circumstance, and is rendered yet more difficult if the individual performing the task is ill prepared.

The adage "Forewarned is forearmed" is accurate when it comes to stress training for police officers. Each and every sensory distortion, shock reaction, startle response, or confusion from inconsistent or incomplete data that an officer or deputy might experience under ambush, or rapidly changing or chaotic conditions, can be prevented by the acquisition of easily taught tools in maintaining concentration and focus of attention, and in critical decision making under stress. While many police commanders will proclaim that they provide that support by giving officers a training class once every two years or so, the reality is that the vast majority of advanced officer training skills are perishable, and show a rapid decline without consistent, monitored practice and repetitive drill.

This type of drill is referred to as **overlearning**. Overlearning has proven to be a highly potent training methodology for the stress environment. Zakay and Wooler (1984) found that training conducted under normal conditions improved performance only under the same conditions, and did not improve performance when subjects performed under time pressure. Therefore, care must be taken that the behavior taught in the classroom setting is the same as that called for in the real-world environment.

As explained earlier, when we first learn to ride a bicycle, we must concentrate upon each element in the skill—otherwise, we will fall. However, as we become more familiar and practiced with the skill, we do not need to think anymore about how to do it; we just do it. This phenomenon is known as **automaticity**. In police work, the term refers to the officer's ability to use tactical actions without the delay caused by shock, perceptual lag, or conscious analysis, because he or she has practiced the skill enough that it has become a conditioned, automatic response.

Skill training in tactical decision making and critical thinking under stress is rarely, if ever, taught to rank-and-file police officers, although Special Weapons and Tactics Teams receive such training and practice as an ongoing feature of their assignment. There is no justification for not providing this training to everyone employed in law enforcement on a consistent and continuing in-service basis. Training in tactical decision making under stress and crisis decision making can be provided to police departments as a "training the trainers" model that can then be inexpensively and continuously conducted by internal police personnel without repeated, outside consultations.

Through consistent practice in scenario-based training, each officer or deputy is tasked with responding to ambush and rapidly changing or chaotic conditions. They continue in the scenario, process the sources of influence in their decision making—i.e., "What am I looking at and why is this important to me?" "It is immensely important that no soldier . . . should wait for war to expose him to those aspects of active service that amaze and confuse him when he first comes across them. If he has met them even once before, they will begin to be familiar to him" (von Clausewitz, in Cannon-Bowers and Salas, 1998, p. 208). Officers who have had such training rarely engage in actions that are not proper and within policy.

Current training in police academies is based primarily in skill-building efforts. There is not really much time available for somewhat broader knowledge training on the theories and issues underlying the skills that trainees are being taught. Just as novice physicians or psychologists are aided by knowledge of the theory underlying the methods they use, so can a novice police person get the benefit of the experts' knowledge by studying theory, without having to learn everything through their own experience.

It is dangerous, as well as false economy, to scrimp on the early education and training experience provided to new police officers and deputy sheriffs. Hours and hours of skill training were unsuccessful at places like Waco, Ruby Ridge, and Columbine. Commanders began the operation with the steps that were supposed to be taken, but then the situations began to change. Application of skill-only methodology resulted in a type of tactical "tunnel vision" preventing the operational law enforcement person from adapting to the new conditions. The result was tragedy that has lived well beyond each incident.

I believe that law enforcement must develop effective mental models to assist police personnel in becoming expert in stress management and decision making, as opposed to just developing procedural expertise. Since a majority of life-threatening police contacts occur in the blink of an eye, most officers and deputies will not have much time to ponder, analyze, and concentrate upon events and conditions. How they are prepared, and the tools, resources, and skills they are provided, will in most cases determine what they do.

Work Fitness

A major piece of the puzzle in developing the best in law enforcement involves the training and education given police officers and sheriff deputies in the initial stages of their career to ensure a high degree of work fitness in all aspects of the role of a police officer. It is common sense that a well conditioned athlete will perform better over a greater breadth of tasks than a poorly conditioned athlete. The same logic is true of police officers. A substantial degree of conditioning and fitness training must continually be provided in mind, body, emotional self-management, and work performance. A person who is physically fit can adapt properly to many more tasks requiring physical effort than one who is out of condition can do. Similarly, the officer who is not expert, practiced, and conditioned to peak performance in decision making under adverse conditions will be unable to respond properly to as many tasks as one who possesses such expertise. These highly perishable skills should be honed continually via regular training and supervision.

A police officer must be trained and conditioned to manage the biological and psychological impact of inescapable work stresses. The longer an officer works in law enforcement, the greater the likelihood that these stresses will have some adverse effect upon his or her work performance and personal life. Traditionally, when this happens, the officer tries to ignore it.

In the Academy, recruits perform a substantial amount of physical agility training and physical conditioning. Thereafter, no institutional or system-wide physical fitness program demands that officers or deputies maintain their physical conditioning throughout their careers and lives. Out-of-shape police officers are dangerous both to themselves and to other officers who may have to rush to their aid. Physical conditioning is crucial to a masterful, professional police response, and should not be cast aside just to lessen risk management concerns about injuries that might occur during conditioning.

Officers and deputies also lack any systematic program of mental and emotional fitness that can carry them through an unexpected crisis circumstance without loss of poise or self-control. Nor are there systematic training efforts in how to recognize and manage work stresses. Police officers are provided little or no training in developing adaptation expertise in their management and control of the body's reactions to alarm, threat, and/or psychosocial stresses encountered over time.

The traditional police habits for dealing with distressing symptoms they begin to experience goes something like this: "If I ignore it and try not to think about it, and no one saw it, then I don't have a problem!" This attitude does not serve officers well, as witness a score of research efforts documenting increased morbidity and mortality directly attributable to police work (see for example, Violanti, Vena, and Marshall, 1986; Fell, Richard, and Wallace, 1980; Everly and Benson, 1989; Blum, 2000).

However, substantial progress has been made in a number of areas of work fitness. Many fewer police officers now spend their end-of-watch transitional period drinking alcohol with their buddies, and many more are engaging in physical conditioning regimens that have been shown to lessen the risk of physical stress problems developing in public safety personnel by ten percent in and of themselves (Blum, 1998). There are simple, easily taught tools and methods to help officers and deputies maintain vigor, health, and well-being through times of stress in their work. Substantial efforts should be initiated to develop mental, emotional, and physical work fitness in police departments as an inherent part of any organizational change efforts.

The price that the public pays for uncontrolled police work stress is an undisciplined, impulsive, or dysfunctional police response that plants a seed for possible tragedy. It is relatively simple to improve work fitness, as it is to develop technology in less lethal tools to permit officers' effective control over resistive or assaultive persons.

While many departments have made psychological and medical services available to police officers, there has been little in the way of programs to transfer these skills from the professional to the police trainer and police expert so that the benefits of medical and psychological knowledge will become integrated within police systems. Work fitness means that police officers will be better capable of performing a wider range of their tasks with skill and demonstrated quality than will those officers not so conditioned. It is time to transfer these skills and support to police officers so that many fewer will be hit by "stones."

Putting it Together

Ultimately, the character, courage, virtue, and ability of the individuals in each position in each police agency—not the rules and procedures written—will determine what actions are taken in the name of the law and its enforcement.

From shortly after his rookie days, Joe had been known as a "cop's cop." He was an active, intelligent, and committed team player who had excelled in police work. To his dismay, however, Joe was injured while on duty, and was forced to retire due to the severity of his injury.

The doctor that the city sent him to had stated that the pain in his arm and shoulder that was so resistant to treatment and rehabilitation was the result of a severe injury to the vertebrae at his neck. The doctor reported to the city that Joe could easily become paralyzed by the slightest physical mishap. Joe was given a medical retirement that he had not sought and did not desire. He pleaded to the risk management personnel of the city and to his command staff not to retire him, to no avail.

He struggled through several months of misery. He knew in his heart that he was born to do police work, as his family had done before him. He tried a number of other jobs, but was miserable not being a police officer. Then it was as if his life began to brighten. He met and married a lovely woman, and found out that she had become pregnant with their first child.

But Joe never stopped trying to return to police work. He had made an appointment with a specialist in the course of one of several appeals he had made to attempt to get his job back as a police officer. The specialist discovered that his earlier medical examination data had been misread. Joe was not as severely injured as was first thought. His city's risk manager agreed to accept this doctor's report that he was fit for duty, and Joe returned to work.

After his return to the agency, Joe was assigned to the Crimes Against Persons detective team. He received a Missing Persons report from a woman whose boyfriend had disappeared. Rather than "kiss it off" as a waste of time (as some other detective might have done with this type of call), he pursued this report with the same "bulldog-like" quality that he applied to everything else. His efforts paid off when he discovered that the missing man's credit cards were being used, and someone was attempting to get cash using the man's ATM card, but the password being entered was incorrect.

When the missing man had not returned in five days, the investigators thought that when he was found they would be dealing with a murder. The next day, the police in a neighboring county stopped a gang member driving the missing man's car. Joe was notified of the arrest. Joe and his partner questioned the gang member for several hours. They learned that two other gang members had "carjacked" the vehicle and kidnapped its occupant. The detectives were now convinced that their missing man was the victim of a homicide, but continued to search for him because the body had not been found.

Meanwhile, the victim of the kidnapping lay upon a carpet, hands and feet bound, eyes covered with several layers of duct tape. He had no idea where he was or why he had been attacked. He believed at each moment that he was going to die. Men had come to his car with guns drawn and kidnapped him. He believed his captors' threats that they would take his body parts one by one to show his girlfriend. The crooks' plan was to demand ransom money from the victim's girlfriend and family, and then kill him anyway to avoid being identified in any manner.

Day 13 turned out to be the break in the case. The victim's girlfriend received a call on her cell phone from a man who demanded ten thousand dollars for the safe return of her boyfriend.

She was allowed to speak with her boyfriend, and by asking him questions that only he would know the answer to, she satisfied herself that he was alive. Immediately, she called Joe for help. Joe's detective sergeant called in all of the undercover detectives, along with the entire robbery-homicide and missing persons unit. Arrangements were made to monitor the phone calls received by the girlfriend when the suspects called to make arrangements for the ransom to be paid.

The sergeant felt overwhelmed by the awesome responsibility of handling this case. He had never handled a kidnapping for ransom case, and neither had any of the other detectives. The sergeant notified his captain, who thanked him for the call but made no effort to come in on a Saturday evening and get involved. The sergeant needed to get ten thousand dollars from a safe, and the off-duty special enforcement detective lieutenant was the only one who could open the safe. This lieutenant agreed to come in and get the sergeant the money.

Joe spoke up and told the sergeant that he did not think it was necessary to give up any money. He suggested that the sergeant handle the exchange of the money and the missing person just like a dope deal. The sergeant had limited experience in narcotics, so he had Joe, an ex-narcotics officer, come up with a plan. It was decided that the money would not be needed. At most they would need a couple of thousand dollars to "flash," but the money would not be given to the suspects until they showed up with the missing person.

The suspects wanted to meet the girlfriend at a hamburger stand, but Joe knew better than to allow the suspects to pick the location. The detectives set up a major surveillance operation at a shopping center. The girlfriend convinced the suspects that she was too scared and nervous to find the hamburger stand's address, so the suspects agreed to go to her location.

One man walked up to the victim's girlfriend as she sat in her car with her window partially rolled down. He asked and argued for the money, and she told him that it was close by and that she would make a call on her cell phone as soon as she saw her boyfriend. At the same time, a second male who had arrived with the first was walking up and down parking rows looking for police. The surveillance team was not spotted, and the girlfriend held her ground on seeing her boyfriend before giving up the money.

The kidnapper told her, "Say good-bye to your boyfriend, then. We will send you one of his fingers for every hour that goes by without you giving us the money." He then left her in the parking lot.

Joe led a surveillance team and followed the crooks as they attempted a number of counter-surveillance actions designed to lose anyone following them. It was a foggy night by this time, and the police helicopter, which was flying without lights in the fog to stay with the suspects, was needed to help the surveillance team. The detectives followed the suspects through a circuitous and complicated route to a motel in another city. They did not have time to contact a judge for a search warrant, as they believed that the kidnappers would now kill the victim for sure if, indeed, he was still alive.

The detective sergeant decided that they could not take the risk of any further delay in police action, because they expected the kidnappers now to kill the victim. The sergeant got together with four of his most trusted detectives, communicated his thoughts to them, and asked for suggestions. The law permits the police to act in exigent conditions in order to directly save life without a search warrant. Therefore, they decided to burst into the apartment with the intention of rescuing the kidnapping victim. With the help of the local police surrounding the motel they had tailed the crooks to, the detectives made an emergency, high-risk entry into the motel room.

They found one crook watching television, and the missing man bound, gagged, and blindfolded on the floor. His captor had been watching the television show *Cops*. The theme song was playing: "Bad boy, bad boy, what you gonna do? What you gonna do when they come for you?" Joe gently lifted the victim and reassured him that he was safe. The kidnapped man told Joe that when the police entered, he had thought that it was just part of the show, as the crooks had watched *Cops* daily while he had lived bound, gagged, and blindfolded. For thirteen days, this man had been terrified that each moment would be his last. Had Joe not led the dedicated group of detectives that never gave up in their urgent quest to save him, the victim's death would have simply been another in a continuing stream of criminality and victimized people. Now, Joe sings, "Bad boy, bad boy, what you gonna do?" and smiles.

The group of detectives sat around the table while I was interviewing them for this book. Their faces were lit by a pleasure of victory that few in law enforcement experience. They had experienced a "once in a career" incident and had directly achieved the salvation of an innocent victim of crime. I could feel the pride they shared in their excellent work.

I recently saw Joe at a conference of outlaw motorcycle gang investigators. He was with his wife and brand-new baby son. His smile of pleasure as he held his son and sang to him the theme song from *Cops* was one of the most heartwarming memories I shall carry with me from this work.

How sad that society is unaware of the continuing heroism engaged in by such men and women of character and worth as Joe and his group of dedicated police officers. With his commitment and determination, his judgment and skill, Joe is a paradigm of the officer who knows what it takes to do it right.

We have an opportunity to support the development, the work, and the health of such heroes, and to fight the trend of mistrust and misunderstanding that endangers their lives and ours. The more we are informed about the realities of police life, and the more intelligently we support police with the proper tools and the proper organizational and social environment in which to achieve excellence, the greater the chance that, when we are in need, someone like Joe will be there.

Bibliography

Baca, Leroy, Sheriff, Los Angeles County Sheriff's Department. Personal communication, 2001.

Bailey, William, ed. *The Encyclopedia of Police Science.* New York: Garland Publishing, 1989.

Bandura, Albert. *Social Foundations of Thought and Action: A Social Cognitive Theory.* Englewood Cliffs, New Jersey: Prentice Hall, 1986.

Bayley, David H. and Harold Mendelsohn. *Minorities and the Police: Confrontation in America.* New York: The Free Press, 1969.

Bildt, Mike. Assistant Chief of Police, San Bernardino Police Department, California. Personal communication, 2002.

Blum, Lawrence. *Force under Pressure: How Cops Live and Why They Die.* New York: Lantern Books, 2000.

——. *Incidence and Prevalence of Work Stress: International Union of Police Associations National Study.* 1998.

Broderick, John J. *Police in a Time of Change.* Prospect Hills, Illinois: Waveland Press, 1987.

Brodeur, Jean-Paul, ed. *How to Recognize Good Policing: Problems and Issues.* Washington D.C.: Police Executive Research Forum; Thousand Oaks, California: Sage Publications, 1998.

Butterfield, Fox. *New York Times,* July 30, 2001.

185

California Commission on Police Officer Standards and Training, *Law Enforcement Officers Killed and Assaulted in the Line of Duty.* 1996, 2001.

Cannon-Bowers, J. and E. Salas, eds. *Making Decisions Under Stress: Implications for Individual and Team Training.* Washington, D.C.: American Psychological Association Press, 1998.

Deuel, Edward, Sergeant, Huntington Beach Police Department, Huntington Beach, California. Personal communications, 1999, 2001.

Everly G. S. and H. Benson. Disorders of arousal and the relaxation response. *International Journal of Psychosomatics,* 36 (1989): 15–21.

Federal Bureau of Investigation, Uniform Crime Report Section, U.S. Department of Justice. *Killed in the line of duty: a study of selected felonious killings of law enforcement officers.* Washington, D.C., 1992.

Federal Bureau of Investigation, *Uniform Crime Reports;* 1994.

Fell, R.D., W.C. Richard, and W.L. Wallace. "Psychological job stress and the police officer." *Journal of Police Science and Administration,* 8 (1980), 139–144.

Friedman, Lawrence M. *Crime and Punishment in American History.* New York: Basic Books, 1993.

Friedman, Warren, and Marsha Hott. *Young People and the Police: Respect, Fear and the Future of Community Policing in Chicago.* Chicago: Chicago Alliance for Neighborhood Safety, 1995.

Friedmann, Robert R. *Community Policing: Comparative Perspectives and Prospects.* New York: St. Martin's Press, 1992.

Geller, William A. and Michael S. Scott. *Deadly Force: What We Know—A Practitioner's Desk Reference on Police-Involved Shootings.* Washington, D.C.: Police Executive Research Forum, 1992, pp.149–150.

Guyot, Dorothy. *Policing as Though People Matter.* Philadelphia: Temple University Press, 1991.

Heal, Sidney. *Sound Doctrine: A Tactical Primer.* New York: Lantern Books, 2000.

Human Rights Watch. *Shielded from Justice: Police Brutality and Accountability in the United States.* Human Rights Watch: New York, 1998, p. 39.

Kolender, William, Sheriff, San Diego County Sheriff's Department. Personal communication, 2001.

Kozlowski, Steve, "Training and Developing Adaptive Teams: Theory, Principles, and Research," in Cannon-Bowers and Salas, *Making Decisions Under Stress: Implications for Individual and Team Training.* Washington, D.C.: American Psychological Association Press, 1998.

Kroes, W. *Society's Victim, The Policeman: An Analysis of Job Stress in Policing.* Springfield, Illinois: C. Thomas, 1976.

Miller, R. K., Huntington Beach Police Department, Huntington Beach, California. Personal communication, 2002.

MSNBC Investigates, "On the Beat in the Los Angeles Police Department," November, 2001.

Narramore, Randy, Chief of Police, Huntington Park Police Department, Huntington Park, California. Personal communication, 2002.

Osuna, Felix, Lieutenant, Santa Ana Police Department; Commander, Special Weapons and Tactics Unit; expert on officer survival and officer tactics. Personal communication, 2000.

Pitman, R.K. "Post-traumatic stress disorder, hormones, and memory." *Biological Psychiatry*, 50 (1989), 450–452.

Polisar, Joe, Chief of Police, Garden Grove Police Department, Garden Grove, California. Personal communication, 2002.

Rosenbaum, Dennis P., ed. *The Challenge of Community Policing: Testing the Promises.* Thousand Oaks, California: Sage Publications, 1994.

Samenow, Stanton E. *Inside the Criminal Mind*, New York: Times Books, 1984.

Sherman, Lawrence W. "Causes of Police Behavior: The Current State of Quantitative Research" *Journal of Research in Crime and Delinquency*, 17 (January, 1980): 69–100.

Simonian, G. "Steve," Chief Executive Officer, Bureau of Investigations, Los Angeles County District Attorney's Office, Los Angeles, California. Personal communication, 2002.

Stonich, William, Undersheriff, Los Angeles County Sheriff's Department, Los Angeles, California. Personal communications, 2001, 2002.

Tobin, Ernest and Martin Fackler, MD. "Officer Decision Time in Firing a Handgun," *Wound Ballistics Review: Journal of the International Wound Ballistics Association*, 5(2001): 8.

Van Der Kolk, Bessel, Alexander MacFarlane and Lars Weisaeth. *Traumatic Stress: The Effects of Overwhelming Experience on Mind, Body, and Society.* New York: The Guilford Press, 1996.

Vila, Bryan and Cynthia Morris, eds. *The Role of Police in American Society.* Westport, Connecticut: Greenwood Press, 1999.

Violanti, J.M., J.E.Vena and J.R. Marshall. "Disease risk and mortality among police officers: New evidence and contributing factors." *Journal of Police Science and Administration*, 14 (1986), 17–23.

Waldman and Cooper, *New York Times*, July 24, 2001.

Walker, Samuel. *Police Accountability: The Role of Citizen Oversight.* Belmont, California: Wadsworth Thompson Learning, 2001.

Walker, Samuel, Cassia Spohn and Miriam DeLone, *The Color of Justice.* Belmont, California: Wadsworth Thompson Learning, 2000.

Wemmer, Richard, Captain, Los Angeles Police Department, Commander, Los Angeles Police Academy, producer of many videotape re-enactments of officer-involved shootings and murdered police officers, expert on officer tactics, officer safety, officer survival. Personal communication, 1999.

Yarmey, A. Daniel. *Understanding Police and Police Work.* New York: New York University Press, 1990.

Zakay, D., and S. Wooler. "Time pressure, training, and decision effectiveness." *Ergonomics*, 27 (1984), 273–284.